FIGHT ON YOUR KNEES

Calling Men to Action Through Transforming Prayer

DR. MELL WINGER, EDITOR

FOREWORD BY DR. JACK HAYFORD

NAVPRESS

Bringing Truth to Life
P.O. Box 35001, Colorado Springs, Colorado 80935

OUR GUARANTEE TO YOU

We believe so strongly in the message of our books that we are making this quality guarantee to you. If for any reason you are disappointed with the content of this book, return the title page to us with your name and address and we will refund to you the list price of the book. To help us serve you better, please briefly describe why you were disappointed. Mail your refund request to: NavPress, P.O. Box 35002, Colorado Springs, CO 80935.

The Navigators is an international Christian organization. Our mission is to reach, disciple, and equip people to know Christ and to make Him known through successive generations. We envision multitudes of diverse people in the United States and every other nation who have a passionate love for Christ, live a lifestyle of sharing Christ's love, and multiply spiritual laborers among those without Christ.

NavPress is the publishing ministry of The Navigators. NavPress publications help believers learn biblical truth and apply what they learn to their lives and ministries. Our mission is to stimulate spiritual formation among our readers.

Cover design and photograph by Dan Jamison
Creative Team: Terry Behimer, Eric Stanford, Darla Hightower, Pat Miller

Some of the anecdotal illustrations in this book are true to life and are included with the permission of the persons involved. All other illustrations are composites of real situations, and any resemblance to people living or dead is coincidental.

Unless otherwise identified, all Scripture quotations in this publication are taken from the HOLY BIBLE: NEW INTERNATIONAL VERSION® (NIV®). Copyright © 1973, 1978, 1984 by International Bible Society. Used by permission of Zondervan Publishing House. All rights reserved. Other versions used include the *New American Standard Bible* (NASB), © The Lockman Foundation 1960, 1962, 1963, 1968, 1971, 1972, 1973, 1975, 1977; *The Message: New Testament with Psalms and Proverbs* (MSG) by Eugene H. Peterson, copyright © 1993, 1994, 1995, used by permission of NavPress Publishing Group; *The Living Bible* (TLB), copyright © 1971, used by permission of Tyndale House Publishers, Inc., Wheaton, IL 60189, all rights reserved; the *New King James Version* (NKJV), copyright © 1979, 1980, 1982, 1990, Thomas Nelson Inc., Publishers; the *Holy Bible, New Living Translation* (NLT) copyright © 1996, used by permission of Tyndale House Publishers, Inc., Wheaton, Illinois 60189, all rights reserved; and the *King James Version* (KJV).

Fight on your knees : calling men to action through transforming prayer
/ compiled and edited by Mell Winger.
   p. cm.
  Includes bibliographical references.
  ISBN 1-57683-352-6
  1. Christian men--Religious life. 2. Prayer--Christianity. 3. Spiritual warfare. I. Winger, Mell, 1954-
   BV4528.2 .F54 2002
   248.3'2'081--dc21

                       2002008208

Printed in the United States of America

1 2 3 4 5 6 7 8 9 10 / 06 05 04 03 02

FOR A FREE CATALOG OF
NAVPRESS BOOKS & BIBLE STUDIES,
CALL 1-800-366-7788 (USA)
OR 1-416-499-4615 (CANADA)

TO DAD

The example of kneeling beside
your bed each night inspires me still.

CONTENTS

FOREWORD

The Reformation didn't end five hundred years ago. No! The Holy Spirit is still unceasingly at work, recovering the sight of God's people from Dark-Age blindness and restoring the power lines that, having been severed, produced centuries of darkness.

This book is about one of the Spirit's foremost re-ignitings. It's about how men are finding the secret to spiritual firepower!

The Reformation has extended onward since its first impact, when the understanding of salvation by faith alone was revived and a clear focus on the Bible's absolute authority reentered the church's life. Since then, reformation keeps occurring, furthering the formation of Jesus' image in His people every time a timeless truth, neglected by unbelief or deadened by empty tradition, is restored to vital life and function among His disciples.

It happened with Martin Luther, and *justification by faith* was recovered to the church's understanding.

It happened with William Carey, and *world missionary vision* was returned to the church's thinking.

It happened with John Wesley, and *a zeal for discipling* was restored to Christian life and practice.

It happened with Charles Finney and Dwight Moody, and *a passion for evangelism* found renewed vigor in the church.

It happened with William Seymour, and a century of *new openness to the Holy Spirit* was begun.

And that brings us to the twenty-first century, as the Reformation continues!

As the Spirit of God worked an awakening of dynamic worship and prayer during the last quarter century, a rekindling of the altar fires of men at prayer has begun—men banding together for spiritual warfare. This book is fuel for that fire. It will be welcomed by men like the hundreds I've watched take up the torch of prayer in my own congregation over the years. These are men who "get it" about prayer, who "grab it" and begin running the race toward spiritual victory the only way it can be run and won—on one's knees.

7

Caught in the grip of a Holy Spirit–inspired awakening of men to their roles

- as godly disciples, without pretense or prissy religiosity,
- as passionate believers, without pushiness or arrogance,
- as loving husbands and caring dads, as well as trustworthy employees and responsible business leaders,
- as interdependent brothers, joined with other men for holy goals,

another step of reformation is taking place. Men are mustering to their role as spiritual warriors, and this book is a handbook for those beginning to report for duty. Doing so calls us men to two basic steps: answering the call and understanding the mission.

Clearly, you have already heard the call or you wouldn't have picked up this book. That call trumpets from 1 Timothy 2:8 (NKJV): "I desire . . . that the men pray everywhere, lifting up holy hands, without wrath and doubting." It directs a man to his ultimate source of power: (1) worshiping God (lifting holy hands), (2) ceasing self-energized conflict (without wrath), and (3) refusing any place to unbelief in God's power and promises (without doubting).

Like the call, the mission is clear, set forth in Ephesians 6:11-12 (NKJV): "Put on the whole armor of God, that you may be able to stand against the wiles of the devil. For we do not wrestle against flesh and blood, but against . . . spiritual hosts of wickedness." From targeting the adversaries and calling to effective equipping, the mission statement concludes by showing *how* battle is to be engaged, through "praying always with all prayer and supplication in the Spirit, . . . with all perseverance and supplication" (verse 18).

So take it from here. And as you do, take your place in the ranks of men who are answering the Spirit's call today and moving forward in the Spirit's power.

A fellow warrior,

JACK HAYFORD
Chancellor, The King's College and Seminary
Founding Pastor, Church on the Way
Van Nuys, California

ACKNOWLEDGMENTS

Special thanks—no, eternal gratitude—goes to my best friend and wife, Paula. She and I both know that without her help this book would not exist.

I want to thank my son Andy for his encouragement and editorial insights, and I want to thank Joe and Elizabeth for their patience and understanding while their mother and I worked on "the book." It's time for a vacation, kids.

Thanks to Terry Behimer of NavPress for her wisdom and help. It was an adventure and a blast to work with her.

And my appreciation goes to the men I pray with each week: Bruce Armstrong, Curtis Bell, Herb Coyer, Jeff Hanks, Scott Kennedy, Chris Kottaridis, and Ward Moore. Their passion to see other men grow in prayer kept me motivated throughout this project.

Freedom Fighters Freedom Fighters Freedom Fighters Freedom Fighters
Freedom Fighters Freedom Fighters Freedom Fighters Freedom Fighters
Freedom Fighters Freedom Fighters Freedom Fighters Freedom Fighters
Freedom Fighters Freedom Fighters Freedom Fighters Freedom Fighters
Freedom Fighters Freedom Fighters Freedom Fighters Freedom Fighters
Freedom Fighters Freedom Fighters Freedom Fighters Freedom Fighters
Freedom Fighters Freedom Fighters Freedom Fighters Freedom Fighters
Freedom Fighters Freedom Fighters Freedom Fighters Freedom Fighters
Freedom Fighters Freedom Fighters Freedom Fighters Freedom Fighters
Freedom Fighters Freedom Fighters Freedom Fighters Freedom Fighters
Freedom Fighters Freedom Fighters Freedom Fighters Freedom Fighters
Freedom Fighters Freedom Fighters Freedom Fighters Freedom Fighters

Part 1:

FREEDOM FIGHTERS

LET FREEDOM RING

Dutch Sheets

"Freedom!"

I'm stirred to the depths of my soul by William Wallace's final word in the movie *Braveheart*. Just before his beheading, he left us a one-word declaration of everything he lived and died for — a lifelong vision and mission statement in a single word. It signifies destiny, duty, patriotism, love, even life itself summarized in one heart-wrenching cry.

I think the scene probably appeals to us men more than to women — at least it did in my house. My wife wouldn't even watch the movie. She'd rather be inspired by something less violent. She also prefers watching figure skating over football, dramas and mysteries over westerns and war movies. Women can be strange.

Back to *Braveheart*. Challenging men to fight for freedom in spite of the risks, Wallace spoke another great line: "Every man dies; not every man really lives." What a statement! He inspired his fellow countrymen to live for a cause, a dream, an ideal. Can you sense God issuing the same challenge to us?

Men who are purposeless merely exist. Their lives make little impact on the world around them. To illustrate the force of purpose, the great Winston Churchill asked, "Why is it the ship beats the waves when the waves are so many and the ship is one? The reason is that the ship has a purpose."[1]

The purpose of this book, men, is to awaken purpose in you— to make you a spiritual freedom fighter. Yes, at the risk of sounding overly dramatic, our goal is to make you a braveheart, a liberator, a nation changer. If freedom is to truly ring in our homes and nation, it will happen only as we take seriously our biblical charge to pray fervently for our nation and our own families.

Robert M. Hutchins said, "It is not so important to be serious as it is to be serious about the important things. The monkey wears an expression of seriousness which would do credit to any college student, but the monkey is serious because he itches."[2]

Sometimes I think we men are serious about too many of the lesser things, scratching too many itches: sports, TV, careers, pleasure, and a host of other diversions. It's time to get serious about spiritual issues, specifically prayer—the aggressive, authoritative kind. The outcome of many battles surrounding us is determined more by our petitions than we can fully understand. The prayers of believers decisively shape families, neighborhoods, and cities. Even the destiny of our nation depends upon our intercession.

Our Freedom Is in Jeopardy

IS OUR NATION'S destiny at stake, perhaps even our freedoms? Are things really that bad in America? Consider these facts and statistics concerning our nation:

- During the twentieth century, the divorce rate rose 700 percent in America.
- Thirteen million children under the age of eighteen are growing up with one or both parents away from home.
- Seventy percent of all juveniles in state reform institutions come from fatherless homes.
- The United States is the single greatest market on the earth for illegal drugs and leads the world in the export of pornography.
- Sixty-six percent of students have sex before leaving high school, leading to more than four hundred thousand teenage

girls getting abortions every year—that's more than eleven hundred each day.

- More than two thousand teenagers a year commit suicide— six each day.[3]

Facing the Facts

These things aren't pleasant to admit and are horrifying to believe, but face them we must. My friend Stephen Mansfield, a Nashville pastor, specifically addresses leaders but speaks to all men as well:

Facing ugly truth is not easy. Often the toughest battle a leader will face is the one against his own reticence to see things as they really are. It requires uncommon courage and very few have the character to deal with such stark reality. But when the truth is known, the worst is over and the benefits are a clearer vision and the wisdom of a "humbler attitude," without which leaders cannot move beyond despair to a brighter day of victory.[4]

For several years, Winston Churchill fought a losing battle in trying to convince England of the true intentions of Nazi Germany. Churchill's repeated warnings went unheeded, and his agony is reflected in these words:

Although the House listened to me with close attention, I felt a sensation of despair. To be so entirely convinced and vindicated in a matter of life and death to one's country, and not be able to make Parliament and the nation heed the warning, or bow to the proof by taking action was an experience most painful.[5]

Referring likewise to the denial of so many, Hitler correctly stated, "What luck for rulers that men do not think."[6]

Facing the Enemy

I'm sounding the alarm, men. I'm asking you to think about the true state of affairs in America. Though it's a war of a different kind, we face an enemy who hates us. Satan wants to steal, kill, and destroy this nation. He wants our families, kids, freedoms, and destinies—and he has made great headway. As the following Scriptures exhort us, it's time to take up our spiritual weapons and fight.

> When I saw their fear, I rose and spoke to the nobles, the officials and the rest of the people: "Do not be afraid of them; remember the Lord who is great and awesome, and fight for your brothers, your sons, your daughters, your wives and your houses." (Nehemiah 4:14, NASB)

> Be strong in the Lord and in the strength of His might. Put on the full armor of God, so that you will be able to stand firm against the schemes of the devil. For our struggle is not against flesh and blood, but against the rulers, against the powers, against the world forces of this darkness, against the spiritual forces of wickedness in the heavenly places. (Ephesians 6:10-12, NASB)

> Be of sober spirit, be on the alert. Your adversary, the devil, prowls around like a roaring lion, seeking someone to devour. But resist him, firm in your faith, knowing that the same experiences of suffering are being accomplished by your brethren who are in the world. (1 Peter 5:8-9, NASB)

> The God of peace will soon crush Satan under your feet. (Romans 16:20, NASB)

> Submit therefore to God. Resist the devil and he will flee from you. (James 4:7, NASB)

God has graciously given us both the ability and the spiritual weapons to win the war against our adversary. But we must take our place in the battle line and fight.

Our Call to Be Watchmen

ONE VITAL ASPECT of our spiritual warfare is captured in the biblical picture of the watchman. In ancient times watchmen were responsible for protecting homes, cities, and nations from those who sought to harm them. They were also to guard crops from animals and thieves.

The nouns translated "watchman" in the Old Testament are derived from three Hebrew verbs: *shamar, natsar,* and *tsaphah.* The various definitions describing a watchman's function help us understand our call to be watchmen. These definitions include the following ideas:

Shamar. "The basic idea of the root is 'to exercise great care over' . . . 'take care of,' 'guard.' This involves keeping or tending to things such as a garden (Genesis 2:15) . . . or it may involve guarding against intruders."[7]

Natsar. "Watch, guard, keep . . . watch over, protect."[8]

Tsaphah. "Look out or about, watch . . . [*tsaphah*] conveys the idea of being fully aware of a situation in order to gain some advantage or keep from being surprised by an enemy."[9]

Like the watchmen in the Old Testament, God is calling men in our generation to take responsibility to protect our homes, cities, and nation from an evil intruder. To effectively guard against the enemy, watchmen must stay awake and be alert. Men, it is our job to prayerfully pay attention so that we're not surprised by the Devil.

This chilling description of the 1986 Chernobyl nuclear disaster illustrates to watchmen the importance of paying attention and remaining alert:

> Two electrical engineers in the control room that night, . . . were "playing around" with the machine. They were performing what the Soviets later described as an unauthorized experiment. They were trying to see how long a turbine would "free wheel" when they took the power off it.
>
> Now, taking the power off that kind of a nuclear reactor is a difficult, dangerous thing to do, because these reactors are very unstable in their lower ranges. In order to get the reactor down to that power, where they could perform the test they were interested in performing, they had to override manually six separate computer-driven alarm systems. One by one the computers would . . . say, "Stop! Dangerous! Go no further!" And one by one, rather than shutting off the experiment, they

shut off the alarms and kept going. You know the results: nuclear fallout that was recorded all around the world, from the largest industrial accident ever to occur.[10]

I'm sure the Holy Spirit has frequently shouted to us, both for our personal lives as well as for our nation, "Stop! Dangerous!" or "Satanic fallout approaching!" It is time that we heed these warnings and rise up to take appropriate action. God is calling us to become watchmen for our nation—spiritual freedom fighters, bravehearts.

Keeping Our Own Gardens

While all of the above definitions of a watchman's function are insightful, the most poignant picture appears the first time any of the three Hebrew words for "watchman" is used in Scripture. As we read in Genesis 2:15, (NASB) God told Adam to "keep" the garden. The word "keep" is the Hebrew word *shamar,* which conveys the concept of protection and preservation.

Adam was assigned the responsibility of being a watchman over the garden. He was instructed to protect what God had given him, to keep it from the Serpent (the Devil). Consistent with His nature to warn, God alerted Adam that he must beware of attacks from the Evil One. Unfortunately, Adam failed in the assignment to protect what God had given him, and consequently he lost his garden.

The Devil is after our "gardens" too—our families, homes, marriages, churches, cities, and nation. Our responsibility as watchmen is critical, as we see in the following story:

In *First Things First,* A. Roger Merrill tells of a business consultant who decided to landscape his grounds. He hired a woman with a doctorate in horticulture who was extremely knowledgeable. Because the business consultant was very busy and traveled a lot, he kept emphasizing to her the need to create his garden in a way that would require little or no maintenance on his part. He insisted on automatic sprinklers and other labor-saving devices. Finally she stopped and said, "There's one thing you need to deal with before we go any further. If there's no gardener, there's no garden!"[11]

Watchmen are gardeners. No gardener, no garden! Let's determine to be gardeners and to keep our gardens—our marriages, children, and nation.

Our Assignment

God has "given" the earth to the "sons of men" (Psalm 115:16, NASB). The Hebrew word for "give" (*nathan*) means not only to give a possession but also to give a charge or assignment. God's gifts are also His assignments and, according to this verse, He has assigned stewardship of the earth to human beings. Part of that assignment for each of us is our family, neighborhood, city, and nation. As men, we must recognize our responsibility to stand as watchmen over these particular arenas.

Unfortunately, the Enemy has already made great inroads into our society. It is too late for us to simply stand guard and keep him out. He's already in. But there is still good news! Although the definitions listed earlier describing a watchman's task refer primarily to defense, there is also an offensive or aggressive aspect of being watchmen. The same three Hebrew words for a watchman's activity can be translated "lay siege to," "spy," and "ambush."[12] Many Bible verses refer to watching in order to overthrow or destroy an enemy (see Judges 1:24; 2 Samuel 11:16; Psalms 56:6; 71:10; Isaiah 1:8; Jeremiah 4:17). God has given us the responsibility of praying authoritatively and expelling the Evil One. Where he has already encroached, we can lay siege to the Enemy's strongholds over this nation and break them.

A Few Famous Freedom Fighters

GOD USED NUMEROUS freedom fighters in Bible times to liberate and change the nation of Israel. Much can be learned about both repossessing and protecting nations by considering a few of these examples.

David: A Model of Passion

David was a freedom-fighting watchman. William Wallace might have drawn his inspiration from this man who conquered giants, took cities, and perhaps more than any other leader in Israel's history, established the presence of God in their midst.

But regardless of whether it was David the warrior, David the worshiping songwriter, David the watchman-intercessor, or David the king, there was one essential characteristic that ran like a thread through every facet of this man's life: passion! To be a truly effective freedom fighter demands that you have passion. Genuine greatness in any area of life, including society-changing prayer, requires us to care deeply.

The world is filled with passionless people without a cause—status quo individuals who go through life making barely a ripple, let alone waves. Someone once jokingly defined status quo as Latin for "the mess we're in." Who can argue with that? And if there is any possibility of changing the messy state of affairs in our land, it will require some King Davids and William Wallaces who care more about souls and eternal destinies than they do about life itself. Spiritual freedom fighters, watchmen who liberate and protect nations, are men of passion.

Mordecai: A Model of Responsibility

Another great watchman in Scripture was Mordecai, the cousin of Queen Esther. Like our nation today, Israel's destiny was at stake. Satan was using the schemes of a wicked man named Haman in an effort to eradicate the Jews. Freedom fighters were desperately needed! Yet through the faith, persistence, prayer, and fasting of Mordecai, Esther, and other Jews, God overthrew the evil plot of Haman and saved a nation.

Listen again to the familiar words of Mordecai to Queen Esther and see an important characteristic of successful watchmen: "If you remain silent at this time, relief and deliverance will arise for the Jews from another place and you and your father's house will perish. And who knows whether you have not attained royalty for such a time as this?" (Esther 4:14, NASB). Notice the blend of faith in God's sovereign ability with the recognition of human responsibility. Mordecai shows us that watchmen who would change nations believe that God *can* if we *will*.

Is it too late for your family and city? Is it too late for our country? Of course not. Not if we believe in our God's ability to do anything and accept the fact that we have come into the kingdom for such a time as this. True freedom fighters are not fatalists; they're optimistic activists!

Gideon: A Model of No Compromise

Another familiar freedom fighter who watched over his garden was Gideon. Once again, Israel was in trouble. Because of the Israelites' sin, the Serpent (the Evil One) had encroached in their garden through a people known as the Midianites. This is the horrible situation described in Judges:

> They [the Midianites] would camp against them [the Israelites] and destroy the produce of the earth as far as Gaza, and leave no sustenance in Israel as well as no sheep, ox, or donkey. For they would come up with their livestock and their tents, they would come in like locusts for number, both they and their camels were innumerable; and they came into the land to devastate it. So Israel was brought very low because of Midian, and the sons of Israel cried to the LORD. (Judges 6:4-6, NASB)

Two important characteristics of watchmen surface in the life of Gideon. First, before Gideon could be used to liberate Israel, he had to tear down the altar of Baal and the idol of Asherah that his father had built (see Judges 6:25-32). Spiritual freedom fighters refuse to tolerate idolatry and compromise of any kind, and they are always willing to start at home.

Following the model of Gideon, we must first deal seriously with any areas where we have personally compromised our commitment to Christ (lust of the eyes, dishonesty, pride, and so on). We who would be watchmen know that we must war against the idols of materialism, greed, and pleasure both in our own lives and in the nation. We realize that our enemies aren't flesh and blood (Ephesians 6:12). We also know that our weapons are spiritual, not physical (2 Corinthians 10:3-5). With these weapons and a conquering spirit, we determine to exterminate encroaching serpents from our lives, homes, and nation.

The second aspect of a watchman modeled in Gideon's life is his willingness to trust God despite overwhelming odds. He was the one, you recall, who was required by God to trim his army from thirty-two thousand to three hundred men (Judges 7:2-8). Spiritual freedom fighters believe that God can save by many or by few. They are not impressed by the size or strength of the enemy, only by their God.

21

We need some Gideons in our land! We need an army of men who will fast and pray—men who will persevere even when their numbers are few. We must have spiritual warriors with great determination to see the idolatrous, garden-devouring serpents removed from their homes and this nation. God is calling each of us to be twenty-first-century Gideons.

Moses: A Model of Starting Over

Of the many other watchmen from Scripture we could mention, Moses is an incredibly important final choice for us to consider. He was, indeed, a liberator, a freedom fighter. "Let my people go" was God's command to Pharaoh through this inspiring watchman (Exodus 5:1). The divine imperative is just as poignant and applicable today as it was millennia ago. "Let my people go" should also be our battle cry as we pray over a generation enslaved in spiritual darkness.

The scene of Moses' life that I want to highlight is his call by God (Exodus 3–4). For forty years, Moses had seemingly lost his sense of destiny and purpose. Indeed, his own failure was the reason. After committing murder (Exodus 2:12), Moses was anything but a leader of God's people. Intimidation, inadequacy, and self-absorption dominated him. Then one crucial encounter with the living God infused him with renewed hope and boldness.

Appearing to him in the burning bush, God commissioned Moses to lead the dangerous mission of liberating His people from Egyptian bondage (3:10). Moses' initial response was "Who am I?" (verse 11). His fear and inadequacy drove him to make a series of excuses not to answer God's call. "Suppose the Israelites will want to know who sent me?" he asked (see 3:13). "What if they won't listen?" was his next excuse (see 4:1). He even reminded the Lord that he was not a polished speaker (see 4:10).

God countered Moses' every objection. Exasperated and out of excuses, Moses blurted out, "O Lord, please send someone else to do it" (see 4:13). That was the bottom line, wasn't it? "I can't, God. Ask someone else."

God finally won the argument by promising to give Moses His presence and power. Now fully empowered, this broken man was transformed into a warrior capable of confronting the most powerful ruler on earth. Like Moses, spiritual freedom fighters are willing to face past failures, fear, and inadequacies and start over.

A New Beginning

CHRISTIAN MEN HAVE to admit that we have been part of the problem. Our apathy, complacency, sin, and prayerlessness have allowed the Serpent into the garden. But it isn't too late. In the words of a famous collegiate basketball coach, Denny Crum, "Most of our future lies ahead."[13]

Thank God for new beginnings, fresh starts! Regardless of your past, you can make a change and not remain imprisoned by your mistakes. Take heart from one who refused to allow his grave failure to derail his future:

> No one imagined that Charles Dutton would have achieved anything, for he spent many years imprisoned for manslaughter. But when someone asked this now-successful Broadway star of *The Piano Lesson* how he managed to make such a remarkable transition, he replied, "Unlike the other prisoners, I never decorated my cell."[14]

Don't decorate your cell! I like Psalm 51:1,10,12 from *The Message:*

Generous in love—God, give grace!
    Huge in mercy—wipe out my bad record. . . .
God, make a fresh start in me,
    shape a Genesis week from the chaos of my life. . . .
Bring me back from gray exile,
put a fresh wind in my sails!

Even if your prayer life has been a failure in the past, men, your future prayer life can be powerful. If the Serpent has encroached in your garden, you can get him out. And together we can run him out of our homes and out of our nation.

"Freedom!"

MEN IN THE TRENCHES

Geoff Gorsuch

L et me tell you a war story. It's the story of an enemy invasion in Vietnam. But it's also the story of how God invaded the lives of a few combat pilots and moved them beyond just saying prayers to really seeking Him in prayer. It's the story of my journey into the presence of God.

You undoubtedly have your own spiritual journey. I hope that, in your journey, you too will find a group of men who will encourage you to keep seeking God. And though the roads we take may differ, life has convinced me that we all share the same crossroads. So, from the heart of one man to another, I offer you the following.

Where I Learned to Pray: "We've Taken a Hit!"

"SAM! SAM! SAM!" the radio squawked.

Our hearts froze. A surface-to-air missile (SAM) was on the hunt. Warnings screamed continuously in my ear as enemy radar went into tracking mode. The red light flashing on my instrument panel told me I had about ten seconds to correctly interpret the missile's trajectory and then "yank and bank" to evade it. But before

I could do that I had to see the missile. And Bill, my navigator seated behind me, made sure I did.

"I see it, I see it!" he shouted over the intercom. "Nine o'clock low."

Sweat burst from every pore as my eyes combed the treetops beneath us. "Where?" I said, my head on a swivel. "I can't see it!"

"Behind us now!" he screamed, unaware of his fear-filled volume. "Bank hard right . . . further . . . further . . . there! See it?"

"No . . . no . . . I got it! I got it!" I yanked the plane into a steep, diving turn. I had just a few seconds left to position us for an evasive maneuver. Still accelerating, belching out a trail of white smoke, the missile was closing fast.

"Jesus," I heard Bill sigh, "save us!"

Our greatest nightmare was now upon us—an antiaircraft missile the size of a telephone pole, filled with the latest technology and "hostile intent." We had only a two-second window to escape—an instant when the missile was too close to correct on our breakaway maneuver but not yet close enough to detonate. If we broke too soon, the missile could still track us. But if we broke too late . . .

"Noowww!" I yelled as I slammed the thrust levers into the firewall. I rolled into the missile's supersonic trajectory and played a lethal game of chicken. For half of those two eternal seconds, I could only watch as death loomed on the windscreen, ready to take the lives of two airmen too young to die. But just before the missile exploded, I rolled the aircraft inverted and yanked it down and away, hoping that the hundred or so feet that now separated us from the missile would also cushion us from its deadly blast.

We held our breath. . . .

Memories flooded my mind with the force of a tsunami: loving parents, Christmas trees, model trains, church, high school basketball, the Beatles, the Air Force Academy, a sports car, pilot training, orders . . . and a war zone.

Then: a flash of light! Memories were immediately shoved aside by the reality of a shooting war, which included a muffled roar, the ping of shrapnel tearing into the tail assembly, a shock wave, the plane twisting out of control, a death grip on the stick, the altimeter unwinding, a cloud of death lingering over us, the earth rising too fast beneath us, and the scream of a man behind me: "Jeeesus . . . save us!"

Fly the plane! I thought in the midst of the chaos. *Fly the plane!* I quickly read the instruments as I wrestled with a sloppy stick. But after a couple of seconds, I realized that though we'd been hit, it had not been fatal. This bird was still alive—and so were we! I kicked the rudder hard to stop the death spiral and restore airflow to the wings. Then, pulling back on the stick, I prayed the tail section could still sustain the g-forces.

"C'mon . . . c'mon . . . c'mon, fly," I whispered as the craft shuddered on the edge of a stall. A second passed. The unwinding altimeter slowed. Another second passed, and the altimeter finally stopped. I held my breath. Another second, and the altimeter started to climb. As I looked outside, we surged through the horizon and shot upward. The rate-of-climb indicator spiked, and a glance back inside revealed that all the other instruments were somehow miraculously "in the green." *If there are no fuel leaks,* I thought, *we just might make it!*

But before I could say it, Bill burst out, "That was beautiful! Wow! What a piece of flying. I can't believe it!" And he went on letting it all out until he finally whispered thanks to the One who really deserved it. But we still had to get home.

Fly the plane!

I turned the mission over to another forward air controller (FAC) to work with the inbound fighters and we headed for "home plate." The tail section had definitely taken some hits. The stick was still sloppy. And the weather had just "crumped." Though it would have been preferable to find an alternate base, I dared not ask more of the plane than it could deliver. We had to get down fast. I radioed, "Mayday! Mayday! Da Nang control, this is Nail. We've taken a hit. How copy?"

"Copy 5-by, Nail," came a soothing female voice.

"I'm in the soup with a wounded bird. Talk me down, sweetheart."

And she did! Through the dark storm clouds that now engulfed us, the air traffic controller guided us until we broke out of the weather just above the runway. The fire trucks waiting for us with their lights flashing would not be needed. As the wheels splashed onto the wet tarmac, we all realized we'd made it home. The training and routine procedures had worked. Once again, death had been cheated.

Or had it?

Why I Learned to Pray: Situation Out of Control!

WE'D SEEN ALL this before. But this time was different. It had all finally gotten to us. When we stepped out of the cockpit and touched the ground, our knees buckled. That's when we knew there had been some "collateral damage." Normally, that meant unnecessary civilian casualties. But our collateral damage was different. We had clearly dodged a bullet—a big one! But we could not dodge its aftermath—we'd been kissed by death.

We'd lost something. We could no longer say that we were *in control*. Youthful dreams had been shattered by reality's hammer. We were only twenty-four, but in just a few minutes of kill-or-be-killed combat, we had aged. We'd lost our innocence, our ability to believe, and we were still too young to take our mortality in stride. And that hurt!

At the debriefing we learned that seven aircraft had been shot down and the toll was mounting. The situation was clearly *out of control*. A huge enemy invasion had been launched and some of our friends had already died trying to stop it. Apparently, it was going to get worse. Much worse. And all that the war zone had to offer to ease the pain was a heavy dose of cynicism and the standard painkillers—sex, drugs, and rock-'n'-roll.

It was Easter Sunday.

A House of Prayer

Bill and I slowly walked back to a string of huts that had been linked together to serve as a barracks in the middle of a hot, humid jungle filled with bats and boas. Let's face it, the "complex" was not the Ritz. But that night, and in the months that followed, it became a house of prayer for twelve men. The pain and disappointment of a Godforsaken war had prepared our hearts to draw closer to God.

In the same violent way Jesus had cleansed the temple in Jerusalem (see Mark 11:15-17; John 2:15), He was now cleansing us. He "overturned the tables" of our self-absorbed dreaming and scheming and "took a whip" and drove the unconscious arrogance of youth out of our lives. As it had been in Jerusalem, so it would now be in Vietnam. Though we still had a job to do and a life to live, God would not let us settle for just a little bit of religious business as usual. He wanted more of us. He wanted better of us. He wanted us holy, free to worship. And He was doing what was necessary to get us there.

All the "thieves" that had been crowding out the true worship of God in the temples of our lives were now, for the most part, gone. And we longed for nothing less than genuine communication with God in spirit and in truth. Clean, honest, humble conversation. No games. No hidden agendas. Just simple obedience.

How I Learned to Pray: The Bible

THE CHAPLAINS WERE so overwhelmed with taking care of the dying and writing condolence letters home that they weren't available to pray with just a few men. We had no chapel and no liturgy to follow. It was all new to us. But we did have our Bibles, and the Holy Spirit pointed us to three men who would guide us into deeper prayer: Jesus, David, and Daniel.

In spite of the war, we sensed that Jesus was preparing us to take our relationship with Him to a new level, if we would only let Him. "Now you are my friends," He said. "I no longer call you servants, because a master doesn't confide in his servants. Now you are my friends, since *I have told you everything* the Father told me" (John 15:14-15, NLT, emphasis added).

Jesus, Our New Friend

Jesus offered genuine friendship to His disciples. And as we studied Him, we began to understand what that friendship meant. It was not a servant-master relationship, living under fear and law. Rather, it was a full partnership. As important as forgiveness was, it was only the beginning. There was a life to be lived together and work to be done together. And to the extent that the disciples were ready to hear, Jesus told them "everything" and invited them to do the same in return. He wanted to be there for them. And now we sensed that He wanted to be there for us as well.

So we told Him "everything": the ups, the downs, and all that lay in between. "Let's tell Him," we used to say. Let's tell Him what we need and ask for help to get it. Let's tell Him how we feel and ask for the grace to deal with it. The point is—let's talk to Him! All

29

He wants is honesty. Authenticity. A real two-way conversation: speaking and then listening. Learning to wait on Him.

But like all guys, we struggled with what to say.

David and the Psalms

That's where David came in. He was a man we could trust. The warrior-poet, who killed Goliath and then went on to become king, knew what it meant to walk with God in the real world. We could understand him. He was a man's man, and yet we discovered in the book of Psalms that he told God "everything." There we found the full range of human experience: joy, sorrow, pain, victory, love, hate, and more. Yet David expressed all of these to God without hesitation or reservation. It seemed reasonable, therefore, to let David, the man after God's heart, show us what to say and how to say it.

So we read the Psalms out loud. In doing so, we'd stop to discuss the prayer, point out its relevance to our situation, and use it to stimulate our own prayers. In the process, we found a pattern that is recognized among men of prayer all over the world today. It is easily remembered by the acronym ACTS, which stands for Adoration, Confession, Thanksgiving, and Supplication. And it looks something like this:

Adoration. When we reflect back to God what the Bible says about Him, we are adoring Him. And David was a master of this. Knowing the attributes of God as well as he did, he said,

> I will praise you, my God and King. . . .
> Great is the LORD! . . .
>   His greatness is beyond discovery! . . .
> He is filled with kindness. (Psalm 145:1,3,17, NLT)

And in Psalm 150 we learned that we should praise God "for his mighty works [and for] his unequaled greatness" (verse 2, NLT). And on it went.

Over time, words such as *awesome, mighty,* and *victorious,* along with *Ruler, Creator,* and *King,* began to appear spontaneously as we prayed. The language that David had used to adore God had started to become our own. Just as we would praise a pilot for a job well done, so we would praise God. Just as we would compliment a friend for his thoughtfulness, so we would compliment God our Friend. But that was only the beginning.

Confession. We discovered that confessing was agreeing with God on what His Word says about us. Confession stops rebellion against God and begins the restoration process. Though we had learned of confession in church, we again looked to David to find out more about it.

Because David was a man of action, sometimes his responses were wrong and even rebellious toward the revealed will of God. As men who, of necessity, had to take responsibility and make things happen, we had no trouble identifying with him. But David's life also taught us that God is always ready to forgive—no matter what!

David had committed adultery, arranged the murder of his mistress's husband, and then covered it all up. When he wrote Psalm 51, he was miserable about what he had done. He started his confession by remembering the basis of all forgiveness—God's unconditional love.

> Have mercy on me, O God,
> > because of your unfailing love.
> Because of your great compassion,
> blot out the stain of my sins. (verse 1, NLT)

David knew that his only hope was to trust in God's love. He went on to pray,

> Against you [God], and you alone, have I sinned;
> > I have done what is evil in your sight. . . .
> Your judgment against me is just. (verse 4)

David did not challenge God's judgment using self-justifying arguments. He repented. And in doing so, the purification process could begin. He continued,

> Remove the stain of my guilt.
> Create in me a clean heart, O God.
> > Renew a right spirit within me. (verses 9-10)

David showed us that all God wants is honesty:

The sacrifice you want is a broken spirit.
A broken and repentant heart, O God,
you will not despise. (verse 17)

We learned that if our sin and separation from God have genuinely grieved our hearts to the point where we are broken by them,
God will forgive. And as we started to come clean, we began to
experience the restored friendship of God. Life looked different.

Thanksgiving. It's one thing to thank God when the times are
good (though we should do just that), but it is quite another to
thank God when they are bad. And things were looking pretty bleak
for us. But the psalmist cut through all that when he said,

I will offer you a sacrifice of thanksgiving
and call on the name of the LORD. (Psalm 116:17, NLT)

A "sacrifice" of thanksgiving is God's challenge to men. It's His
way of preventing self-pity and whining. We knew it. And we
believed it. But at times doubt crept in.

So the question became "Can we find something to be grateful
for anyway?" And that's how we began to "thank God anyway." We
started with the obvious: our health, the safety of our families, and
the freedoms we cherished. But as the thanksgiving list length-
ened, we noticed that our focus shifted off the war and back onto
God. The exercise wasn't easy to do, but as we entered "into His
gates with thanksgiving," we saw that "the LORD is good" (Psalm
100:4-5, NKJV).

His mercy is everlasting,
and His truth endures to all generations. (verse 5, NKJV)

And that was something to be thankful for!

Supplication. We were stunned at how boldly David asked
God for help. At times we had the impression that he even
demanded vindication! Though it took us a while to get there,

we began to ask God to act on our behalf as well. Like David, we too could pray with confidence facing a war.

> Hear me when I call, O God of my righteousness!
> You have relieved me in my distress;
> Have mercy on me, and hear my prayer. (Psalm 4:1, NKJV)

> I come to you for protection, O LORD my God.
>   Save me from my persecutors—rescue me!
> If you don't, they will maul me like a lion.
>   (Psalm 7:1-2, NLT)

The cry of David's heart was not only for physical deliverance from his enemies but also for psychological and emotional deliverance from his wartime afflictions. How we identified! And how many we knew who had survived the war, only to be defeated by post-traumatic stress or "painkillers" that had torn their souls apart. We prayed for them by name and then went on to pray for each other, our families, our friends, governments, and peace.

What to Expect in Prayer: His Presence—and Peace!

THAT'S HOW THE Psalms taught us to pray. Divine words from the divine Book said it all to God in a way that honored Him and ministered to us. As we adored God, we recognized His place in creation and ours as His creatures. Confession was our way of acknowledging that God had the right to set the standards and hold us accountable. We then learned to thank Him not only for His salvation but also for everything around us that we took for granted. In these ways our hearts were prepared to ask according to His will. And we did—specifically!

But what to expect as an answer from God eluded us. Should we expect God to do what we ask Him to do? In spite of all the verses that affirmed that concept, for some reason it seemed presumptuous to us. We were just too inexperienced to know, until we discovered Daniel and the unique answers he received to his prayers.

Daniel's Intercession

Daniel had a right to complain, but he didn't. The Babylonians had invaded his country, killed many of its leaders, and taken Daniel and other princes as hostages back to Babylon. For years after, they were trained to serve a corrupt kingdom, and because they had no choice, they did so with distinction. Through it all, however, Daniel prayed.

Though he had remained faithful to God, he found that his people had not. The corruption of Babylon had been too much for them, and so Daniel, broken by their disobedience, fasted and prayed (Daniel 9–10). He adored God and thanked Him for all His goodness to His people. But then he began to confess his sins and the sins of his nation: "We . . . are covered with shame because we have sinned against you. . . . Open your eyes and see our wretchedness. . . . We do not ask because we deserve help, but because you are so merciful. . . . O Lord, listen and act!" (9:8,18-19, NLT).

Daniel's prayer became our own.

He wanted God to change the circumstances, right the wrongs, and restore His people's dignity by setting them free from the bondage of Babylon. He had reason to expect this because of the prophecies of Jeremiah. So, in humility, he expected God to do what he had asked. But God did something else first. He touched Daniel!

Using Gabriel as messenger, God reached down, not to change the circumstances, but to be a friend and to explain everything to Daniel (Daniel 9:22-27; 10–11): "Daniel, I have come here to give you insight and understanding . . . for God loves you very much" (9:22-23, NLT). God's immediate priority was not the circumstances but the man.

God wanted to give Daniel insight and understanding to face the realities of his life. And what's more, He wanted to strengthen Daniel for what was to come: "O Daniel, . . . understand the words that I am about to tell you and stand upright. . . . Do not be afraid, Daniel, for . . . your words were heard, and I have come in response to your words. . . . Peace be with you; take courage and be courageous!" (Daniel 10:11-12,19, NASB).

God's answer to Daniel's prayers was Himself!

The Results

In the past we'd been told that there were only three answers to our prayers: yes, no, and wait. Our experience, however, taught us that there was a lot more to prayer than asking and receiving. God will respond to our needs as we ask Him. He eventually did set Daniel's people free to return to the Promised Land. But in the process, another dimension of prayer emerges—the presence of God Himself.

As it had been for Daniel, so it was for us. Our times of prayer were characterized by "the peace of God, which surpasses all understanding" (Philippians 4:7, NKJV). There were moments of sorrow and moments of joy. But most of all, we took courage from our Friend.

When God entered the room, we all sensed it. No one wanted to talk. As caught up as we were in a technical world, we could *feel* His presence as He filled us with the courage to face it all one more time. God was there for us, undeserving as we were.

It was God. No doubt about it. We just knew. His divine personality, the Holy Spirit, communed with us and we became convinced that, in spite of it all, life had an answer. And the Answer revealed Himself to us, over and over again, as He had always promised to do. "You will seek Me and find Me when you search for Me with all your heart" (Jeremiah 29:13, NASB).

A Final Word

SO THAT'S THE story.

It all started on Easter Sunday 1972 in a war zone far from home. But all of us who transformed that barracks into a house of prayer so long ago are still seeking God. Oh, we're not perfect, and we don't pretend to be. Since then, we've "taken some hits" and the situation has at times been "out of control": sickness, business reversals, struggles with marriage, and the like—the crossroads we all share!

But through them all, the Bible has continued to show us how to enter into His presence. And we have found that He always has been there for us. His peace, perspective, and power have enabled us to "get the plane home" one more time. And looking back on it all, I wouldn't trade that for the world.

A SOLDIER'S ENTANGLEMENTS

Dale Schlafer

Thinking about the title of this chapter reminded me of an experience I had thirty-three years ago. My wife and I had just become the proud parents of our first child, a daughter, whom we named Tracey. My wife was going to a meeting at church and I was to stay at home to take care of Tracey. This was the first time I had taken on this responsibility alone; nevertheless, I felt supremely confident about my ability to handle it. After all, I was the adult.

Things went splendidly until it was time to get the baby ready for bed. I filled the little tub on the changing table, took my daughter's clothes off, and placed her in the water. We had a great time until I began to wash her, using a little cake of soap I found close by. Somehow her hands got in the soapsuds, and then she touched her eyes with her soapy hand. She started to scream, which precipitated the following chain of events.

So surprised was I by the screaming that I dropped Tracey into the tub, causing her head to go under the water. This led to more ear-shattering screams. I reached for a towel, but instead of getting the towel, I proceeded to knock the light off the table, plunging the room into darkness. I now had a soapy, wet, screaming baby in my arms and couldn't see a thing.

I reached for the light switch, but just at that moment Tracey wiggled, causing me to lose my balance momentarily, crashing me into the card table where we kept all the baby supplies. The card table then collapsed, sending pins, lotion, and cotton balls all over the wooden floor. I was now holding a screaming baby in the pitch dark, trying to work my way out the door and into the bathroom. As I took a step, I slipped on the spilled lotion, my feet went out from under me, and I landed on a safety pin that was lying open on the floor. I was now lying in a pool of baby lotion with a soapy, screaming baby in my arms, in pitch darkness, with a safety pin sticking out of my posterior.

That's what I thought of when I read the word *entanglement*. On the day of my first solo fathering experience, I was all caught up in lotion, cotton balls, safety pins, and a screaming baby. All of these things kept me from doing the task of getting my daughter ready for bed. In the same way, there are all kinds of entanglements that keep Christian men from having a prayer life that really makes a difference. The most common I've observed are ignorance, intimidation, innocent pleasures, and unresolved issues with our earthly father.

Ignorance of Prayer's Real Nature

FOR MANY MEN, what hinders prayer is ignorance of just what exactly prayer is. Most men know enough to assume that prayer is addressing God, but after that, it gets fuzzy. Prayer is first and primarily a relationship with the Father, Son, and Holy Spirit. The Lord actually desires to spend time with us! The apostle Paul wrote, "I want to know Christ" (see Philippians 3:10). Notice he didn't say, "I want to know *about* Christ." That is not to say that gaining knowledge about Jesus Christ is a negative endeavor. On the contrary, it is an important part of a man's discipleship. But Paul wanted us to understand that we can know Jesus Christ in the same way that we can know a human friend.

In fact, the word "know" in Scripture is often used for sexual intercourse — the most intimate knowing possible. This is the kind of intimacy that the Lord wishes to have with us. It is not sexual at all, but rather God desires to spend time with us in an intimate setting and intimate way.

If prayer is indeed part of a relationship, then it follows that it is conversation, which means we do not do all the talking. What kind of marriage would you have if you did all the talking and your wife never uttered a word? It certainly would not be a relationship! Similarly, when we pray, we are to both talk and listen to God.

As mentioned in the Psalms, we are "to inquire in his temple" (27:4, NKJV). One of the purposes of prayer is to get God's perspective and direction for our life. Inquiring presupposes that there will be an answer. Each morning, we need to get God's marching orders for that particular day. We must listen to what God wants to say as we pray.

A while back, I was with some South American pastors who made an incriminating observation about the way we North Americans often approach God. One of them explained, "You open your meetings with a short prayer. Then you make your plans and decisions and ask God to bless them. You don't even give Him a chance to tell you what *He* wants!"

This pastor's words came as a real rebuke to me. We should listen and obey as we pray, and not merely speak to God regarding the concerns on our heart. As we worship the Lord in prayer, we get our directions for living. What we do is a result of our time spent with Christ in relational praying.

Prayer is also a way to give and receive love. This is a hard one for many of us men. In fact, some of the literature that I have been reading on men's ministry suggests that we should stay away from the subject of love for God altogether. The so-called experts who write these books contend that because the Bible often uses feminine terms to refer to the relationship between God and the church, it is too confusing for men to understand. To this I reply, "Bunk!"

When asked what was the greatest commandment, Jesus replied, "You shall love the LORD your God with all your heart, with all your soul, and with all your mind" (Matthew 22:37, NKJV). Rather inclusive isn't it? As followers of the Lord Jesus Christ, we don't have an option here. Yes, it does take prayer and thought to understand, for example, how we as men are "the bride of Christ." It's hard for us to put on a bride's dress, especially when white isn't one of our colors! But this is not rocket science. We can understand how Jesus, the Bridegroom, loves the bride, which means He loves us. Especially if we are married, we understand this relationship. So please don't tell me that men can't understand God's love or that we can't, in a masculine way, love God as well.

I remember the first Promise Keepers conference held in a stadium. Twenty-two thousand men showed up. I was talking with my son when suddenly, from one side of the stands, I heard: "We love Jesus. Yes, we do. We love Jesus. How 'bout you?" I looked up and watched the most amazing thing transpire. The other side of the stadium responded, only louder, "We love Jesus. Yes, we do. We love Jesus. How 'bout you?" With each antiphonal response, the volume grew louder until it was almost deafening. Twenty-two thousand men were telling each other, God, and anybody within a mile radius that they loved Jesus! I am quite sure that until that moment most of those men had never been so loud or enthusiastic about their love for Jesus. Up to that point, they had not known that it was appropriate for them to do that.

Telling God of our love is not just for crowded stadiums. Just as those men were unashamed to tell the world of their love for God as a group, so we need to tell our heavenly Father of our love as we pray individually. A fulfilling experience in prayer is hearing God say, "I love you," and telling Him, "I love You, too." As simple as this sounds, our churches are filled with men who are unaware of the intimate side of prayer.

Innocent Delights and Their Deadening Effect

IGNORANCE, HOWEVER, IS not the only issue that keeps us men from praying. John Piper has said, "It is not the banquet of the wicked that dulls our appetite for heaven, but endless nibbling at the table of the world."[1] Satan can do much to keep us from becoming all that Christ desires. Sinful choices like adultery and addiction to pornography can certainly keep us from a vibrant prayer life. But I'm convinced that many men battle a more subtle entanglement than gross sin. Their prayer lives are weak due to the distraction that can come with God's good gifts.

I find interesting what Jesus described as keeping us from His banquet. It comes out in a parable in which several men are invited to dinner at the home of their friend. Their reactions may seem surprising.

> "They all alike began to make excuses. The first said, 'I have just bought a field, and I must go and see it. Please excuse me.'
> "Another said, 'I have just bought five yoke of oxen, and I'm on my way to try them out. Please excuse me.'
> "Still another said, 'I just got married, so I can't come.'" (Luke 14:18-20)

You see, the greatest adversaries to our love for the Lord are not His enemies but His gifts. It is the pleasures of life that choke out the Word of God (see Luke 8:14). Now, understand that the pleasures of life and the desire for other things are not, in themselves, wrong or evil. But brother, when the gifts begin to obscure our relationship with Christ, then something is amiss. Eating food, biking, watching TV, playing sports, exercising, surfing the Internet, talking on the phone, pursuing hobbies, studying, or reading mystery stories (all good gifts) can become hindrances to our prayer life. God has created us men to be *doers*. We like projects and tasks, and there is nothing wrong with that. But when we spend more time nibbling at the table of the world than at the banquet table of our God, our prayer life will be affected negatively.

If we don't take time to "be" with the Lord, then we will be caught up in the rat race of our day and begin to lose our sensitivity to Christ's presence. We must not allow ourselves to become entangled by distractions. The Lord encourages us, "Be *still*, and know that I am God" (Psalm 46:10, emphasis added).

Intimidation by Other Believers

THE THIRD HINDRANCE that holds men back from praying is intimidation. All Christians struggle at times with this debilitating influence. The word *intimidate* literally means "to make timid." Timidity is crippling to our spiritual development. Some men become so discouraged through feelings of inadequacy that they throw in the towel. Comparing ourselves to others sets us up to be intimidated. The Bible calls us unwise when we measure ourselves by those around us (see 2 Corinthians 10:12).

Sometimes a wife may intimidate her husband when it comes to prayer. On numerous occasions, men have said something like this to me: "I really am growing in the Lord, especially in prayer. But my wife has been a growing Christian for years. She spends hours with the Lord. I will never catch up with her, and I'm afraid to pray with her because she is so advanced. What should I do?" That is a great question.

Brother, if this is your situation, first you need to thank the Lord for your wife and her walk with Christ. She is God's good gift to you. Likely, the Lord answered her prayers when He got hold of you. The second thing you need to understand is that you will never catch up with her spiritually. If you did, it would mean that she had stopped growing in the Lord, and you don't want that. Third, you must take the lead and pray with your wife (see Ephesians 5:23-30). God has made you the leader of your family, and as far as this responsibility goes, the degree of your spirituality does not matter. Further, a godly wife will be thrilled to have your leadership, because most likely she has been praying for it.

My wife is very experienced in prayer. There are those in the church who, I believe, have a special call to labor in prayer, hearing and seeing things that the rest of us do not. My wife is one of these. So when I lead her in prayer each day, it can be an intimidating experience unless I remember that she truly wants me to take the lead. This is what God has asked me to do. Further, as a man and as one gifted differently than my wife, I need to remember that I won't pray the same way she does.

Intimidation doesn't come just when men pray with their wives. When we look around at how other men pray, we can easily spot those who pray more eloquently or with greater authority than we do. This can leave us with a vague notion that God ranks us on our performance in prayer. Actually, God delights in our humble utterances offered in faith, regardless of their degree of eloquence. When feelings of intimidation begin to erode your desire and confidence in praying, remember, "God did not give us a spirit of timidity" (2 Timothy 1:7). That's a promise you can stand on!

Unresolved Issues with Our Earthly Father

ANOTHER HINDRANCE THAT keeps men from praying effectively is an unresolved relationship with their earthly fathers. This issue is so critical because our relationship with our earthly father directly impinges on our relationship with our heavenly Father. I would go so far as to say that this is one of the greatest reasons that men struggle in prayer.

When I do men's retreats, I always begin with this subject because the problem is so pervasive. I have discovered that easily more than 50 percent of the men at *every* retreat have to do business with this issue in some manner. A man should be able to look to his earthly father for significance, security, and love. When that occurs, a boy grows to become a healthy man. When it doesn't happen, it affects every aspect of his life, not just as a child but as an adult.

For example, listen to what the actor James Caan said about never hearing his dad say, "I love you":

> In retrospect, I never knew how to deal with success. Maybe that goes back to my childhood, to my father. He was a German Jew, a tough man who worked as a butcher. I never saw my dad cry once in my life, not even when his own mother died when I was seven. (That macho thing.) I loved him to death, *but he never said he loved me. So I never felt worthy. I think it just drove me to succeed to get his approval.*[2]

My guess is that there are thousands of Christian men — indeed, some of you reading this page right now — who find themselves in the same condition as Caan. As a result, how does such a man react when he hears that God loves him and wants to spend time with him? He can't accept it as fact because his earthly father never did this. He feels that he must earn God's approval and love. On top of that, there are legions of men whose fathers failed in every area of upbringing or abandoned them, and as a result the sons are still irate. This deeply affects a man's relationship with God and hinders his prayers.

There is an answer to this tragic situation. For those of you wounded by your earthly father's failure to give you significance, security, and love, the answer must begin with forgiveness.

Scripture tells us in numerous locations that not to forgive is a sin. "Forgive us our debts, as we"—as we what?—as we "forgive our debtors" (Matthew 6:12, NKJV). If you struggle in your relationship with your earthly father, listen to me now. It's time to forgive your dad. Here's what I want you to do: Tell your heavenly Father, right now, that you forgive your earthly father for either failing you or forsaking you as well as for the other things you hold against him. I know this is hard, but you need to release this burden you have carried all these years. The next thing to do, assuming that your dad is still alive, is to make an appointment with him to tell him that you have forgiven him. During this time, you need to ask any clarifying questions you might have. In most instances, there will be a wonderful reconciliation, but not in every case. Let me remind you that you are not responsible for your father's response, just for your own.

If your father is dead, I want you to write a letter similar to the following. As you read what this man said, imagine the release he experienced as he wrote of a painful past:

> Dad, you've been dead over twelve years. Kissing your cold, lifeless forehead at the funeral home and saying "goodbye" are still vivid memories to me. It was too late then to reveal many things on my heart. This letter is to say what I wasn't able to express at that time.
>
> I went to the family farm today and buried some things that represent sad memories and bitter feelings. An old fishing lure, a baseball card, an empty beer can and a rusty nail from the barn. The old fishing lure, because you always went fishing with your friends but never once with me. The old baseball card, because you never took time to show an interest in things I enjoyed. The old beer can, because it represents the heartaches your habitual drunkenness brought to me and the family. Waiting for you in the car for hours in front of the bar still haunts me. The old rusty nail, because it symbolized Christ's death in dealing with all the sins and pains from the past. Colossians 1:20 (NKJV) states, "And having made peace through the blood of His cross."
>
> Dad, I did this to forgive you through the work of Christ on the cross . . . to bury the difficult past . . . to obtain freedom from

it . . . to embrace the peace that has eluded me all these years. Dad, I'm sorry. I forgive you. I love you. Your son, Doug[3]

Can you sense, even through the printed words, the freedom this man has now that he has forgiven his father? Don't wait any longer. Forgive your father now! Discover a whole new relationship with your heavenly Father.

Throw Off Entanglements

AT THIS POINT, you may be asking, "How can I minimize all these issues and maintain a healthy prayer life?" Two components of prayer enable us to throw off and be kept from entanglements. In fact, these two aspects of prayer are the keys to gaining and keeping a revived relationship with Christ.

Repentance
The first ingredient is repentance. Repentance is changing your mind, turning from sin, and dedicating yourself to the amendment of your life. *Repentance* is not a popular word today. We would much rather talk about recommitment and rededication than about repentance.

But you see, the Bible's message is repentance, not rededication. Jesus preached repentance in His earthly ministry (Matthew 4:17) as well as His glorified ministry (Revelation 3:19). I like what Richard Blackaby said: "The proper response to disobedience is not a commitment to try harder, but brokenness and repentance for rejecting the will of Almighty God. God looks for surrender to his will, not commitment to carry it out."[4]

I have found that it is much easier to understand repentance through the use of the following words: *revelation, recognition, remorse,* and *resolution.*

- Revelation is what happens when you are reading the Bible, listening to a sermon, talking with a friend, or reading a book and you suddenly grasp a truth of God that you had not understood previously.
- Recognition is when you realize that this truth is describing you or your situation.

- Remorse is being sorry that you have failed your heavenly Father in this regard, which leads to confessing it as sin and asking for God's forgiveness.
- Resolution is the determination not to do again that which you have just confessed. It is an act of the will to go in the opposite direction.

Let me give you an illustration to cement this concept in your thinking. Do you remember the old TV program *Wide World of Sports?* "The thrill of victory and" — and what? That's right — "the agony of defeat." What was the picture that represented the agony of defeat? You remember! Yes, it was the ski jumper crashing off the side of the ski jump.

Did you know that he did that on purpose? I found that out just a couple of years ago. Here is how it happened. During the day, the sun had come out and melted the snow on the ski jump. With the late afternoon shadows, the temperature began to plummet. The melted snow turned to ice. As the skier began his run down the jump, he recognized that something was terribly wrong. He was traveling at a rate of speed that would propel him off the jump with such velocity that he would clear the landing area, crash into the trees, and perhaps be killed. I want to suggest to you that he repented. Stick with me now.

- First, there was revelation: *This is ice.*
- Second, there was recognition: *I could be killed.*
- Third, there was remorse: *I knew I shouldn't have jumped today.*
- Fourth, there was resolution: *I won't jump. I'll just fall off the edge of the ski jump.*

I trust that you will never again forget repentance. But brother, it is not a laughing matter. Repentance is the way to rid yourself of the things that entangle you. It is the way to reenlist as a freedom fighter, as Dutch Sheets talked about in chapter one.

Brokenness
The second ingredient a Christian needs in order to throw off and be kept from entanglements is brokenness. King David said,

> The sacrifices of God are a broken spirit;
> a broken and contrite heart,
> O God, you will not despise. (Psalm 51:17)

Brokenness means "altered by breaking." *Contrite* means "shattered." These two words express a concept that God wants us to understand: To be broken and contrite is not to be weak.

Think for a moment about a wild horse. For a horse to be useful to us humans, it must be "broken"; that is, it must learn to obey its master. When the horse is finally broken and trained, it can be trusted to respond to the slightest command of the rider. The horse's only desire is to do what its master says.

That is why we need the continual attitude of brokenness and contrition, so that our sinful, willful lives can be reformed and remade into the image of Christ. As we make it our intentional habit to pray, "God, show me to me as You see me," the Holy Spirit helps us to see where we have sinned and failed our Lord. We then have the opportunity to repent and choose to live through the power of Christ in a different way. As we pray like this, we will discover more and more power to live in a manner that honors Him and accomplishes much for His kingdom. Why? Because according to Scripture, only cleansed hearts have power with God (Psalm 66:18; Hosea 10:12; James 5:16). Brokenness and contrition are God's wonderful gifts to us for a powerful life in the battle against the world, the flesh, and the Devil.

It's Never Too Late

I DON'T KNOW how old I was when my father and I no longer kissed one another or said, "I love you." I imagine I was around seven or eight. The Schlafers are from good German stock. When we shake hands, we want no other body parts touching, and we shake standing as far away from each other as possible. My Dad never said, "Let's not kiss anymore or say, 'I love you;'" it just happened.

I never doubted my Dad's love, and he was a wonderful father, but as far as demonstrating and speaking of our love, we simply didn't do it. This behavior continued until I was twenty-five years old. One afternoon I went over to my father and said, "Dad, I have to do this for myself." I threw my arms around his neck and kissed him and said, "Dad, I love you." He started to cry and returned my kisses, saying, "I love you, too." From that time on, until my Dad went to be with Jesus, we kissed every time we met, as well as when we parted, and we always said, "I love you."

Now there was not one unmasculine thing about our relationship. It was simply a father and son expressing their love in an appropriate manner, making our relationship deeper and better. I don't know all the psychological and cultural reasons why my dad and I were cheated out of almost twenty years of expressing our affection and love. However, one thing I do know is that we didn't let it remain that way. We chose to take the corrective steps that allowed us to have ten years of being able to express our love for one another—ten years that I wouldn't trade for anything.

Man of God, I don't know what has kept you from a close, warm prayer life with your heavenly Father. But I encourage you to take whatever corrective steps are necessary to move into a deeper relationship with your Father in heaven. Remove those entanglements as an act of your will and find your Father waiting to love you as a son.

Part 2

STRATEGIC BATTLEFRONTS

Strategic Battlefronts Strategic Battlefronts

WARRING FOR THE FOUNDATIONS

Wesley Tullis

A ll men are passionate about something. Be it sports, music, business, or hunting, something sparks a fire within us. Having grown up in Louisiana, I've got duck hunting in my blood. Oh, for ponds encircled with ice and the smell of marsh gas and sludge—all for the sight of green heads pitching into your decoys at the break of day! Face it, guys, we have passions, and many times they aren't rational! We were created by God to have passion, and our battle is whether or not we will have misplaced passions.

For more than two decades, I have been involved in mobilizing Christians to pray for and establish churches among the unreached peoples of Islam, Buddhism, and Hinduism. I contended for years that the war of the ages was getting the gospel where it isn't. But I am now convinced that the war of the ages is not evangelism or church planting but rather maintaining passionate intimacy in three major areas of our lives: with God as Father, with our family, and with accountable friends. When these fires of passion and intimacy are in the foundation of our life, they will result in an overflow of all kinds of world-changing ministry.

Since the fall of man (Genesis 3:6-7), God has been on an unalterable course to restore His original will and ways on earth. The intensity and fury of His commitment to do so is seen immediately after humanity's fall. God prophesied that His Son would one day die an excruciating death on the cross and thereby "crush" His enemy's head (Genesis 3:15). Key Scriptures in the first few chapters of Genesis reveal His original intent: "Let us make man in our image, in our likeness, and let them *rule*" (1:26, emphasis added).

The tone of God's heart is unmistakable. We men are called to have dominion, to conquer, and to reign. The entire earth is our field of operation. This is not a job for the passive or irresponsible. Men struggling with a victim mentality (Genesis 3:12) or shame (verses 8-10) will find it difficult to rule. We need to refuse daily to give in to passivity, victimization, and shame so that we can take up our spiritual responsibility to rule rather than be ruled by our weaknesses.

Genesis 2:15 is the second verse revealing God's original design for establishing His authority and reign on earth, and it falls squarely on the shoulders of men: "The LORD God took the man and put him in the Garden of Eden to work [cultivate] it and take care of [guard and watch over] it."

What are we to watch over? What are the foundational issues we as men are to guard and preserve? The answer to these questions goes to the root of all personal and social issues. How men fulfill their role as watchmen will determine whether our nation will flourish or deteriorate. God's original design for you and me is to be passionate, alert watchmen over six major "gardens," which I refer to as the "Foundations of Integrity for Authentic Success."[1]

In this chapter I will hit only the first three foundational gardens, all related to intimacy: with God as Father, with our family, and with accountable friends. These deal more with who we *are* than what we *do*.

More Flak When You Are over the Target

FLAK IS ANTIAIRCRAFT fire. Recall the classic World War II movies with bombers moving in on their targets. Picture the strategic gas refinery coming into the cross hairs of the bombardier, and then the

52

entire aircraft being rattled by the intensity of the explosions of flak. The closer they get to the target, the greater the flak!

The more we focus on this core issue of men awakening to their godly responsibilities, the more "flak" from the Enemy starts exploding around us. Over the past twenty years, leaders such as Ed Cole, Pat Morley, and Coach Bill McCartney have taken men's ministries to new heights in unity and national impact. The growing "call to war" movement is also making the Enemy nervous, because men are rallying around their pastors and uniting in aggressive prayer.[2] The following statistics reveal how hard the Enemy is attacking men in order to disconnect them from God's original design to rule and watch over the earth:

- 9 out of 10 people arrested for drug abuse are men.
- 8.8 out of 10 arrested for drunk driving are men.
- 9 out of 10 arrested for serious crimes are men.
- 7 out of 10 who fail one or more grades in school are male.
- 8 out of 10 who commit juvenile crimes are male.
- 7.5 out of 10 who commit suicide are men.
- 7.5 out of 10 patients in mental institutions are men.[3]

What I love about God's surpassing wisdom is that He shows us what is of utmost importance by allowing the Enemy to overplay his hand. In this case, I believe the Lord is directing us to pray for the restoration of men to their rightful place as His watchmen. This is because of the influence and authority He designed men to have. Consider these statistics:

- Win 100 children to Christ — get 3.5 new families in church.
- Win 100 women to Christ — get 17 new families in church.
- Win 100 men to Christ — get 93 new families in church.[4]

These figures are not meant to say that it's more important to lead men to Christ than to lead women and children. They simply reveal the impact a godly man can have. When I was attending Church on the Way in Van Nuys, California, I heard Dr. Jack Hayford say numerous times, "As the men go, so goes the church." I would add, As the church goes, so goes the nation.

Authentic Success

IN *HONEST TO GOD?* Bill Hybels shares, "Authenticity means consistency—between words and actions, and between claimed values and actual priorities. . . . I believe the greatest challenge facing the church during the next two decades is the disease eating away at its power and integrity—inauthentic Christianity."[5]

A few years ago, the Lord led me on a twenty-one-day partial fast to pray about these key foundations or gardens. I was crying out that God's grace would make them more real in my life. A week into the fast, I received a call that forever changed my life.

My friend's voice broke as he told me that his only son had just committed suicide. I'll never forget the heart-wrenching agony of looking into that casket three days later.

The previous year, this man had been consumed with making millions of dollars in his business. But like each of us fathers, he would have traded all of his outward success for the life of his son. In an instant, this tragedy confronted him with the questions *What are the most important things in my life? What am I giving my life to?*

I can't get that open casket out of my mind. I can still hear the mother's uncontrolled wailing and the father's deep, sorrowful sobs. An ancient Chinese proverb says, "Sorrow is defined by a father looking into the grave of his son." That day, the conviction for these foundations of intimacy was burned deeply into my heart.

All of us have known of men who, on the outside, had all the appearance of success: best-selling authors, gifted ministers, powerful politicians, and successful businessmen. But something cancerous was eating away from the inside out, and they began to collapse. Maybe it was immorality, pride, greed, or deceit. It's time to raise up a generation of men who have foundations of integrity and who will plant seeds to impact future generations. We need to resist any allurement to live for ourselves, becoming a one-generation wonder.

Let's explore these foundations one at a time.

Foundation 1: Intimacy with God as Our Father
Jesus was the perfect model of manhood, depending completely on the Holy Spirit. His example is not meant to condemn us; rather, it

is to emphasize our desperate need for the Holy Spirit to empower us to be like Him.

The first recorded words of Jesus could not be more emphatic. He underscored the necessity of living in intimacy with God: "Why were you searching for me?" Jesus asked His earthly parents. "Didn't you know I had to be in my Father's house?" (Luke 2:49). Three verses later we see that "Jesus grew in wisdom and stature, and in favor with God and men" (verse 52). This was the fruit of living with God as Father. Having a close relationship with the Lord supplies us with everything we need to be authentically successful in life.

Jesus' life reflected the longing of God's heart for intimate, worshipful friendship: "True worshipers will worship the Father in spirit and truth, for *they are the kind of worshipers the Father seeks*" (John 4:23, emphasis added).

If we men do not find our heartfelt needs of acceptance, significance, and identity met through our relationship with God as our Father, then we will be constantly trying to meet them by what we do (work, position, titles). We will be tempted to fill this God-size void with things of this world, which the Bible categorizes as "the lust of the flesh, the lust of the eyes, and the pride of life" (1 John 2:15-16, NKJV). Gordon Dalbey writes,

> Christianity is a relationship with the living Father God. It's God's answer to the deepest longing in a man's heart. . . . Jesus' saving work in men is prompted, therefore, not by the shame which makes us strive to do right, but by the grace which allows us to be real. It's sustained not by trying to measure up, but only by confessing that we can't. It proceeds not from a determination to do the right thing, but from a longing to know the true Father. A real man is a man who's *real*. And only real men can lead us into this new covenant manhood—men who have dared to cry out in their own inadequacy and surrendered it to Jesus for Him alone to bear.[6]

All of Scripture is about a loving Father who passionately desires relationship with sons and daughters. The call to spend time with Him in prayer is not an order to add another item to our to-do list but rather an invitation from our Father's heart to share all that He is with us.

In Luke 15 a father pleads with his older son, who had faithfully obeyed everything he commanded but totally misunderstood his father's heart of grace and generosity (verse 28). As a picture of God's heart, this father looks into his son's angry yet dutiful eyes and says, "My son, you are always with me, and *everything* I have is yours" (verse 31, emphasis added).

Are you hungry to discover *everything* God has for you? Then set a time and place each day to plunge into the adventure of knowing God as your Father. Psychologists say it takes twenty-one days to form a habit. Therefore, in less than a month, you could be enjoying a dynamic new friendship with the Lord, because your quest lines up with Jesus' sacred request. He expressed it in John 17:26: "I have made you [the Father] known to them, and will continue to make you known in order that the love you have for me may be in them and that I myself may be in them."

Here are a couple of Web sites where you can download helpful resources for this journey: www.thewpc.org and www.theamen.org.

Foundation 2: Intimacy with Your Family

The next garden of utmost priority that we are to watch over is our family. Men, if we try to find our significance and identity outside of our relationship with our heavenly Father, we will tend to trample our wives and children in the process. We will make our business or ministry our mistress. So let's say we have the root issues of significance and identity in check (which is a lifelong endeavor). Then the ongoing war will be one just to stay on top of our hectic schedules in order to keep our family a priority.

Derek Prince tells the story of a minister who was asked his opinion of a certain person: " 'Is he a good Christian?' The minister replied, 'I don't know; I can't tell yet. I haven't met his wife.' That was a wise answer! A husband's success is seen in his wife."[7] This reflects an old Jewish adage regarding men: "I know how much you love God by looking in the eyes of your wife!"

But it is not only our wives who serve as a gauge of our character. Our children, too, reflect how well we are doing in our God-given role as men. Absent and neglectful fathers, in particular, can inflict great harm on children—and the effects of that harm show up in important ways.

Millennia ago, Plato observed, "The saga of a nation is the saga of the family."[8] All we need to do to know the significance of our impact as fathers is to look at our society. Fatherless daughters are 111 percent more likely to become pregnant as teenagers, 164 percent more likely to give birth to an illegitimate child, and 92 percent more likely to fail in their own marriages. Fatherless children are two times as likely to drop out of high school, 50 percent more likely to have learning disabilities, and 100 to 200 percent more likely to have emotional and behavioral problems, according to the National Center on Health Statistics.[9]

The most reliable predictor of crime is neither poverty nor race but growing up fatherless. Fatherless sons are 300 percent more likely to be incarcerated in state juvenile institutions. "This trend of fatherlessness," says David Blankenhorn, founder of the Institute for American Values, "is the most socially consequential family trend of our generation."[10]

The Bible also confirms the magnitude of a father's influence. Genesis 18 and 19 provide insight into the lives of two men: Abraham and Lot. How they dealt with their families affected the destiny of a city and God's purposes for generations.

Have you ever wondered why God chose Abraham from all the inhabitants of the earth to be the father of the nation of Israel? He and Sarah were desert nomads, an older couple far beyond retirement age. What was the critical factor in God's selection process that caused His global surveillance satellite to beam in on this man Abraham? The answer is found in Genesis 18:19: "For I know him, that he will command his children and his household after him" (KJV). A key reason God chose this man was because He knew Abraham would take his place of authority in his home. God knew Abraham would cultivate and keep this garden called his family, not just for one generation, but also to "his household after him" — his grandchildren. The end of verse 19 seals the importance of Abraham making his family a priority: "that the LORD may bring upon Abraham that which he hath spoken of him." God had declared that in Abraham "all the nations of earth will be blessed" (Genesis 18:18).

As if to put an exclamation mark on the revelation God is conveying to us about the importance of family, when reading Genesis, we leave Abraham and move right into the life of Lot. Lot's story illustrates what happens when we don't have the right priorities or foundations in our lives.

"The two angels arrived at Sodom in the evening, and Lot was *sitting in the gateway of the city*" (Genesis 19:1, emphasis added). The gate of the city was the place of political authority, a strategic spot for a godly man to be. And yet the rest of the chapter reveals that Lot had wrong priorities. It is obvious from Lot's legacy that he did not instill a love and reverence for God in his home.

How can we deduce that? His future sons-in-law thought he was kidding when he warned them to leave the city (Genesis 19:14). Lot himself hesitated to leave and the angels had to drag him out (verse 16). His wife turned back to gaze at Sodom in direct disobedience to the Lord (verse 26). His two daughters got him drunk and had sex with him (verses 30-38).

If Lot had been watching over his own home, he would have had five righteous people under his direct influence. If their lives had influenced only four others, then the entire city would have been spared. God promised not to destroy the city if ten righteous people could be found (Genesis 18:32). One godly family could have saved a whole city from destruction. Instead, Lot was found at the gate of the city, not at the gate of his home. What a clear case of misplaced focus!

These illustrations underscore the truth that it is critical to our nation for Christian men to strengthen their families. The A-men Project is a growing national movement that is helping men take action to see a reformation in their households.[11] Here are the commitments they have adopted:

- Pray daily with your wife. When couples pray daily together, only one out of a hundred divorces.[12]
- Guard the Sabbath in your home. When we take one day a week to rest, the level of peace greatly increases in our homes.
- Pray with your children and lead them in reading the Bible.
- Train your children to have devotions.[13]
- Bless your children regularly.[14]
- Be proactive. Establish a mission statement for your family, including ninety-day goals for each member.[15] If you ran your business or ministry like you managed the purpose,

vision, and mission of your home, would you be operating in ninety days? in a year?

All this is crucially important. Yet to live a life that makes a difference, we can't stop with simply establishing devotional and family patterns. We need to give to and receive from godly brothers.

Foundation 3: Intimacy with Accountable Friends

The call to men in this hour is a call to war in the trenches of real life. And that means having accountable friendships. That means connecting with other men in a small group.

Every Wednesday morning, from 5:00 to 7:00 A.M., I colead a men's group. Seven of us began meeting two years ago, and now it averages close to seventy each week. Staying on focus with our foundations of integrity is the reason we get together. There have been times when I didn't think I could make it, but I have been carried by these friendships. The deep camaraderie that is built when men are together in the trenches is incredible.

I think of times like the premature birth of our youngest son, Daniel. The doctors couldn't tell us whether his lungs would function on their own when the respirator was removed. The love and prayers of my brothers strengthened my faith, and we saw a miraculous healing in our son's lungs.

When I have been at my weakest, the support of these men has impacted my life with a healing power almost equal to the heavenly Father's. For most of us men, it will be the unconditional love and friendship of other men that will heal our wounds related to our earthly fathers.

As we have met weekly for prayer, we have seen countless miracles of men's lives transformed. Here are just two:

- A top executive whose marriage was on the rocks trudged into our gathering while his wife waited in the car in the early morning darkness. By the end of our time of ministry, he was fully restored with his wife, and two years later, they are touching many other marriages as a couple transformed by Jesus' redemptive power.
- One man who started attending was under a restraining order

and had received divorce papers. His wife saw the changes in his life after he attended the group for a few months. She chose to renew her vows with him at our 5:00 A.M. meeting!

The ground rules for our gathering are simple: honesty and humility before God and each other. We have a sincere desire to see each other be truly successful through fulfilling our destinies. God's presence consistently shows up there because He "gives grace to the humble" (Proverbs 3:34; James 4:6). We incorporate the following components:

- sharing God's Word and life experiences as they relate to being overcomers in the foundations of integrity
- vibrant worship to connect our hearts to the Father (we ask for His light and presence to come and speak to us personally about our foundations)
- honest communication and prayer in groups of two or three
- powerful, united prayer for our churches, city, nation, and global issues

We experience great authority and faith in prayer because of the renewed intimacy with the Father and with each other. Ninety percent of the time I do not feel like getting up to join my brothers when my alarm goes off at 4:00 A.M. What are you going to do to change your lifestyle so that you can connect with other men in the "trenches of warfare" called life? You, too, may need to sacrifice sleep to meet with brothers.

The Power of Proactivity

MEN, WE NEED to have a proactive attitude and establish intentional habits that line up with these three foundations. Paul Lewis, in *Five Key Habits of Smart Dads*, shares insightfully,

> The proactive father refuses to let what happens (or happened) to him rule his life. He does not let either the present or the past dictate the future.
>
> When you are a proactive father, you choose your response to problems so that you can fulfill your fathering responsibilities.

... The reactive father's vocabulary is replete with "I can't . . .
I have to . . . I can't help it . . . I must." The proactive father, on
the other hand, uses phrases like "I can . . . I want to . . . I will
. . . I choose to . . . "

A proactive father shelves all the excuses. . . . He believes
his true priorities will determine the course of his life, because
he is *tenaciously* deciding to keep those priorities in line.[16]

"Tenaciously" sounds like warfare to me! "The kingdom of
heaven has been forcefully advancing, and forceful men lay hold of
it" (Matthew 11:12).

This challenge to be proactive convicted me deeply when our
fifth child was born. I took action and mapped out my weekly activities, my 168 hours, in my Get Real Planner. I ended up resigning
from two national leadership positions to make sure I realigned my
life with these foundations.

I would like to tell you that this was an easy decision, but I had
to go through some honest soul-searching. Giving up those positions
touched the unholy chord in me that seeks to get my identity and
significance from my performance. But the decision has certainly
paid off.

God Is Up to Something

BROTHER, I WISH we could be sitting across from one another, eye
to eye, just as I do with men every Wednesday morning. We know
these foundations are God's will. The breakdown in obedience
occurs not because pastors, leaders, and ministries are not proclaiming this message but rather because we are not getting in the
trenches of daily life to wage war and to watch over the precious
gardens of life that God has given to us.

Dennis Rainey, in *One Home at a Time*, gives an impassioned call
to revival and reformation in America. He says,

The only true reformers in our day will be common men and
women with . . . uncommon courage . . . dads and moms, singles and single parents who will ignite the fire of personal reformation, regardless of the cost. The battle must be fought up

close, heart by heart, marriage by marriage, home by home, community by community.[17]

The tide is turning! The power of God's Spirit is being released as never before to turn the hearts of the fathers back to their children (see Malachi 4:6). There is a fresh grace for men to take their place of spiritual authority and responsibility.

Men are gathering in small groups throughout the nation to wrestle with the daily challenges of being a true worshiper of God, a godly husband and father, and a man of integrity in the marketplace. Listen to the sound of God's Spirit moving on men across our nation:

- The Southern Baptists had men's ministries in approximately 18,000 churches in 1999—double the number from five years earlier.
- The Assemblies of God has 6,000 men's ministries (in 1996 they had 1,200).
- The United Methodists have 8,000 men's ministries.
- The Church of God has 2,000 men's ministries.
- The Evangelical Free denomination has 650 men's ministries (in 1996 they had only 312).[18]

Referring to this exploding men's movement, Crawford Loritts of Campus Crusade for Christ said, "We're living in an exciting time. There is a movement. I don't yet want to call it an awakening or mass revival, but God is stirring the waters and has been for 15 or so years."[19]

Let's jump into these "stirring waters." As more of us say yes in this hour and return to foundations of authenticity, vitally connected to our local churches, and united with the churches across our communities, we will see God's authority and power unleashed in our nation as never before. Let us be men who have a passion to see a reformation of our nation—a reformation that explodes from the inside out, a reformation founded on God's will and ways. Then His reign and glory will cover the earth as the waters fill the sea (see Habakkuk 2:14).

Come on in—the water's fine!

ENSURING DOMESTIC TRANQUILITY

Randy Wilson

L isa sat straight up in bed, muffling a scream. She was drenched in sweat and could hardly speak. Finally she whispered, "Randy, Randy!" and began to weep. I reached for her trembling body and held her close. She slowly began to tell me about the recurring dreams—dreams of my walking out on our one-year-old marriage.

You see, Lisa's family has a history of men abandoning their wives and children. They have left a sad legacy of shattered lives and betrayal. Until the dreams began to pummel her, we had no idea of the Enemy's goal to enslave her heart with fear of abandonment. Lisa had been waking up and fighting alone in prayer for months. But on this night she called on me to battle for her.

I began to pray for God's presence to fill our bedroom and His peace to replace the fear in Lisa's heart. That night, as I called out to God on Lisa's behalf, He answered. The nightmares stopped immediately, and Lisa no longer fought those tormenting thoughts.

Twenty years and seven children later, the pilgrimage of prayer for Lisa and me continues. It has been a journey of wonder, faith, and total abandonment to God. The glorious mystery of one flesh that Paul described in Ephesians 5:31 has been magnified in our marriage through seeking the face of God together and relentlessly beseeching Him to bless our children and the future generations. This is a sacred quest that captures God's heart for all Christian marriages. For as Doug Wendel aptly noted, "Our God, an intimate God, has designed us to relate to Him with the person who is most intimate with us."[1] What an awesome thought that God created us and brought us together to seek Him as a couple in this journey of life!

Setting the Stage

THE ICE SKATING clips of the husband-and-wife team Ekaterina and the late Sergei Grinkov illustrate the dynamic design of couples united in prayer. (I know, I prefer the NFL's greatest hits too, but just stay with me for a moment.) This is a profound picture of strength, glory, and unity flowing together. The strength of Sergei supporting Ekaterina on the ice, lifting her above his head, carrying her with amazing balance and fortitude, is incredible. Ekaterina glides in harmony with him, complementing his strength with her own strength, beauty, and grace. To flow as one, Sergei and Ekaterina must completely trust each other. What a picture of teamwork in marriage!

This illustration also portrays a husband and wife's teamwork in prayer. A couple's prayer, like ice skating, requires trust, harmony, and complementary gifts. Notice the synergy produced when the Grinkovs blend their gifts and strengths. Skating alone, they could never produce the same splendor they did as a team. Sometimes I think our heavenly Father must marvel at a couple's united prayers with the same sense of pleasure that we have when we view Olympic skaters.

It is important to note that Jesus defined the basic prayer unit as "two of you."[2] He said, "I tell you that if two of you on earth agree about anything you ask for, it will be done for you by my Father in heaven" (Matthew 18:19). I believe God designed this dynamic, basic prayer unit as a means to fulfill His purposes and bless families. How awesome that God set the required minimum number at two, not seven or eight! Notice the power—"anything you ask for, it will be done." Notice the requirement—"if two of you on earth agree." When we unselfishly agree with God's will, this little unit is packed with power. No wonder Satan resists the simple act of a couple kneeling together!

Guidelines for Praying as a Couple

THE FORMAT AND structure for praying together as a couple can be relatively simple. In fact, complicating the process may cause you to abandon the whole venture. Cheri Fuller shares these words of wisdom for getting started:

> Make a commitment to pray together every day for a month . . . and watch what happens. Pray about whatever is important to both of you—each other, your kids, jobs, finances . . . areas of stress, and needs. For some couples, praying before getting out of the bed in the morning is the best time; for others, before going to sleep at night works better. Whatever the time, make it a priority . . . and stick to it.[3]

To develop and maintain a satisfying prayer experience, remember the following basic guidelines:

- Keep it brief at first (even just a few minutes).
- Be yourself (your wife knows when you're not).
- Be consistent in order to develop the habit.
- Ask forgiveness of your wife before you pray, if you know you've offended her.
- Set a specific time for prayer but also develop a climate of spontaneous prayer throughout your day (pray in the car, over the phone, or as you take a walk).
- Begin your prayer time with thanksgiving and praise.
- End by speaking a blessing over each other, such as "Father, thank You for giving my wife strength, health, and grace for everything she needs today. I bless her in the name of Jesus."

The War Zone of Oneness

NOW THAT I have set the stage for the power and design of united prayer in marriage, let me tell you about the struggle involved. I have encountered many spiritual land mines that have discouraged, distracted, and thwarted my attempts to pray with my wife. Let me share with you some common challenges men face as they venture into this war zone of oneness.

Land mine 1: "My wife knows I haven't been much of a leader in the family. She sees all my weaknesses. How do I initiate prayer with her when I have failed her as a leader?"

Unfortunately, men fail their wives in a myriad of ways, ranging from a thoughtless word to infidelity. In between lie broken promises, financial irresponsibility, and emotional neglect. Perhaps you've left it to your wife to discipline the kids, and she feels overwhelmed. Maybe she works outside the home and resents your reluctance to help with household chores. Whatever the situation may be at your house, if you're like me, you've made a mistake or two over the years.

Because I did not have a father or another male role model growing up, for years I felt inadequate as the leader of my own family. I scrambled to catch up with Lisa spiritually and looked desperately for a model I could emulate. I pursued friendships with older men who were the kind of husbands and fathers I wanted to become. I invited them to lunch and pumped them with how-to questions. Through these relationships and studying God's Word, the Lord answered my cries for help.

God led me to key principles in James 5:16: "Confess your sins *to each other* and pray *for each other* so that you may be healed. The prayer of a righteous man is powerful and effective" (emphasis added). I began to humble myself, confessing to Lisa and God my failure as a husband and the leader of my family. God showed me that my prayers were powerful and effective, and I began to believe it! I was motivated to make praying with my wife a priority, and I started seeing tangible answers to prayer. My relationship with God and Lisa grew stronger as a result. Ed Cole has observed this same truth: "I was amazed to discover how inconsistently men pray with their wives. They evidently don't know the scriptural principle that *prayer produces intimacy*. You become intimate with the one *to* whom you pray, *for* whom you pray and *with* whom you pray."[4]

Nevertheless, there are still times when I need to humble myself before Lisa, telling her one more time that I blew it and asking her forgiveness. But sometimes I have let pride get the best of me, rather than walking in humility. Pride can kill oneness and destroy relationships we hold dear. In the book *Praying God's Word*, Beth Moore exposes the pitfalls of pride:

> My name is Pride. I am a cheater. I cheat you of your God-given destiny . . . because you demand your own way. I cheat you of contentment . . . because you "deserve better than this." I cheat you of knowledge . . . because you already know it all. . . . I cheat you of holiness . . . because you refuse to admit when you're wrong. . . . I cheat you of genuine friendship . . . because nobody's going to know the real you. I cheat you of love . . . because real romance demands sacrifice. . . . My name is Pride. I am a cheater. You like me because you think I'm always looking out for you. Untrue. I'm looking to make a fool of you.[5]

Don't let pride make a fool of you and cheat you out of the richness of life God offers. The key to ongoing tranquility in the home is to ask forgiveness as soon as the Holy Spirit tells you that you blew it.

Pride may have the power to destroy us, but a humble spirit brings us honor (see Proverbs 29:23). Men, God is all about our success as husbands. He has made a way for us to flourish in our relationship with our wives, but we must choose to humble ourselves. Confession and a contrite heart bring us into God's presence and restore unity with our wives. By faith, take a deep breath and speak the words "Honey, will you forgive me?" I guarantee she'll then be happy to pray with you.

Land mine 2: "Sometimes I am disappointed because I feel nothing when I pray with my wife."

You would think that praying with your wife would produce a sense of the Lord's approval and blessing. The reality is that sometimes I sense God's presence when I seek Him with Lisa—and other times I don't. As Lisa and I have journeyed together in prayer, there have been times when I've struggled with the questions *Am I touching the throne of God? Is this activity making any real difference?* But Ephesians 3:12 assures me, "In him and through faith in him we may approach God with freedom and confidence." The access doesn't come through feeling, circumstance, or any particular form of worship; it is simply through faith in a holy God.

In their book, *Thirty-One Days of Prayer*, Warren and Ruth Myers write,

> If [God] makes us particularly conscious of His presence, let's enjoy it. And if the Spirit carries us along in prayer, let's be grateful. But if not, we can still pray, depending on the Word, like the jet pilot who depends on what the instruments say rather than how he feels. We can't judge the success of our prayers by our emotions. And we're not to let our emotions determine whether or not we pray.[6]

In my case, I grew up in a family strong in doctrine but weak in understanding the Spirit's power in prayer. I saw prayer as a formality, modeled only before a meal and at church on Sundays. As a result, ingrained in my memories are cold, lifeless prayers without much meaning or freedom. Therefore, I struggle in trying to touch God with my emotions.

I've been encouraged through the example of Hudson Taylor, the missionary to China who received amazing answers to prayer. The story is told, "Someone asked him late in life if he always felt joyful when he prayed. He replied that his heart usually felt like wood when he prayed and that most of his major victories came through 'emotionless prayer.'"[7]

Your faith alone accesses the inner court of heaven. Your faith alone will defuse this land mine of being disappointed by a lack of emotion in prayer. To effectively pray, we must enter into utter abandonment of self-absorbing thoughts and embrace a deeper trust in God's Word. That's because "without faith it is *impossible* to please God" (Hebrews 11:6, emphasis added).

Land mine 3: "I feel self-conscious praying with my wife. I feel freer praying with other men than I do praying with her. She seems to clearly express in prayer what I can't."

Remember, men, your wife is called to help and complete you. She is God's special gift to you (see Proverbs 19:14). Instead of bristling at her ability to enter into prayer with ease, embrace her gift and listen attentively to her heart. Lisa explains that my reassuring presence with her in prayer actually liberates her to fully express herself.

William Grunall's words are helpful to struggling men: "Sometimes you hear another pray with freedom and fluency, while you can hardly get out a few broken words. Hence you are ready to accuse yourself and admire him, as if the gilding of the key makes it open the door better."[8]

Sometimes a husband and wife simply have different prayer styles. These insights from Cheri Fuller can bring couples into a more powerful prayer union:

> Sit down with your spouse and talk about your different gifts, prayer styles, and approaches to prayer. Maybe one of you likes to use a prayer list, while the other likes to feel led by the Spirit. Perhaps one of you is more emotional and prays heartfelt prayers, while the other is more analytical. . . .
>
> Whatever your prayer styles, accept each other's differences. Realize that if God wanted you to pray exactly the same way with the same style and gifts, you wouldn't need each other! Discussing your differences and thanking God for them is a first step toward melding them in prayer.[9]

Land mine 4: "When I pray with my wife, a combustion in our relationship suddenly happens. A fight will come out of nowhere and derail all attempts to go forward in prayer."

I can't begin to tell you the number of times this scenario happens. I hear this same story from guys across the country as we talk about building a lifestyle of prayer in our homes. It's not a coincidence. It comes from living in the Enemy's camp. We must not shrug off the fact that all hell is against marriage! One thing I have learned is that if you don't fight *for* your wife, you will fight *with* her.

Determining to pray is critical, but the plan goes out the window if I'm not being sensitive to Lisa. She closes her spirit and clearly is not ready to enter into prayer. Resentment also comes when our communication has suffered due to a stressful, over-packed schedule. I can prevent this combustion by simply taking her into my arms and asking her how I can meet her needs. Then we are ready to enter into God's presence together.

Hopefully, this insight exposes Satan's strategy to make you and your wife enemies. The next time you sense the Evil One stirring up strife, step into your position of authority, be sensitive to your wife's heart, and stand fast in the heat of the battle.

If an explosion occurs as you begin to pray, listen to your wife's needs and press into prayer. Don't let the Enemy win by derailing you from your mission to pray.

Satan uses this simple tactic of inciting disharmony because he understands the scriptural principle that a husband's prayers are not just an isolated activity; they are an extension of his daily relationship with his wife.

The apostle Peter addresses this issue: "Husbands, in the same way be considerate as you live with your wives, and treat them with respect as the weaker partner and as heirs with you of the gracious gift of life, so that nothing will hinder your prayers" (1 Peter 3:7). The Enemy knows that the way a man treats his wife actually enhances or hinders his prayers. Where Satan sees a little strife, he agitates it and effectively disables God's basic prayer unit of two in agreement.

In *The Complete Husband* Lou Priolo exhorts us to relate to our wives by feeding them with our presence, caring for them with our love and gentleness, and nourishing them with our words and kindness.[10] Men, how are we nurturing our wives as heirs to the gracious gift of life? How are we tending her heart, understanding her, and accepting her as God's perfect helpmate for us? I urge you not to quickly skip over these questions; remember, your prayer power may be at stake.

Land mine 5: "Prayer can be laborious."

If you say that prayer takes great effort, you're in good company. At times, King David moaned about prayer as well:

> Be merciful to me, LORD, for I am faint. . . .
> > My soul is in anguish.
> > How long, O LORD, how long? . . .
> > I am worn out from my groaning;

all night long I flood my bed with weeping
and drench my couch with tears. (Psalm 6:2-3,6)

There are times when Lisa and I have persevered in prayer and
did not receive an answer to a specific request for days, weeks,
months, even years. Darkness and silence from God are passages of
great pain that Lisa and I have had to pray through. We have learned
that God is somehow testing us in those quiet and dark places. We
found this verse to be life changing during the seasons of heart-
wrenching turbulence when God called us to simply cling to Him:

Who among you fears the LORD
    and obeys the word of his servant?
Let him who walks in the dark,
who has no light,
trust in the name of the LORD
    and rely on his God. (Isaiah 50:10)

Are we willing to seek the Lord when there seem to be no
answers, no light, no open doors, no revelation, and no vision? Are
you willing to cling to Him with relentless perseverance, knowing
that He is faithful and hears every word? As Rabbi Shmuley Boteach
says, "Success . . . is not about victories, but about perseverance."[11]
    A great story of perseverance comes from the life of Walter
Payton. He ran nine miles during his football career and was knocked
down every 3.8 yards by a man twice his size.[12] He just kept getting
up. He kept running. He kept his eye on the goal. He kept focused.
He endured the pain and never gave up in the middle of the battles.
This is what manhood is about! Perseverance takes courage. Laboring
in prayer takes unbridled commitment. God will do the rest.

A Strategy for Maintaining a Peaceful Home

IN ADDITION TO establishing a consistent prayer time together, we
must also be proactive in making our home a refuge of peace. We must
maintain the deep conviction that "as for me and my household, we
will serve the LORD" (Joshua 24:15). Men, God has placed the ultimate
responsibility for the protection and peace of our homes upon us, not

our wives. We either let the Enemy reign or we take our place and execute our authority in Christ. *Executing*, not just *exercising*, my authority as head of my home brings peace. Let me share with you a personal journey that happened a few years ago.

Our family had moved to a new home in San Antonio. Within the first week, I noticed that the children were very unsettled—a change from their usual peacefulness. Lisa began to exhibit signs of depression and confusion. She couldn't think clearly, she would weep for no apparent reason, and even simple tasks like going to the grocery store would put her in a state of confusion and fear.

These behaviors were out of character for my wife, who is decisive and has a deep walk with God. So, as Lisa was spiraling downward, we began to seek God for answers.

A few days later, a neighbor ventured over to introduce himself. He asked if we were enjoying our new home and then described the family that had just moved out. He told us that violence and rage filled the house constantly. The domestic outbursts would often bring the police to their door. The neighbors would see things flying out the window, and before long clothes and household items would litter the yard. He finished his story by saying he was grateful we had moved in.

We had our answer! The house needed to be spiritually cleansed, dedicated to God, and prayed over. I immediately called Lisa and the children together to pray. I anointed the door posts and windows with oil. Praise and worship music filled the home as we went room to room boldly declaring, "This home is under the authority of the Lord Jesus Christ." By faith, we prayed that the Enemy would no longer reign and roam freely!

Lisa was instantly freed from the oppression she'd been experiencing, the children settled into a quiet peace, and God's presence filled the house.

Men, I was already positionally the authority, as head of my home. Now God called me to *execute* His authority in the domain of my responsibility. As men, our number-one place to wage war is in the home, not in the marketplace. However, the way we execute our authority at home flows into our work arena. Personal authority is birthed in the secret places with our wives and children. Our position of authority *outside* the home only comes from authentic personal authority *in* the home!

Ever since our experience in San Antonio, wherever we have lived, we have determined to dedicate our home to the glory of God. Here are some specific strategies God has led us to use:

- Along with our children, we walk the boundaries of our property. We call out to God to establish His presence there, to reign, and to use us to bring about His kingdom purpose.
- We anoint every room with oil, praying for God to cleanse any defilement and evil. We also expect Him to show us anything that needs to be thrown away because it doesn't glorify Him. This includes any inappropriate books, CDs, games, or videos. Then we end by asking God's Spirit to bring divine power and peace.
- Sometimes we have a more formal dedication, inviting our pastor and other believers to join us in blessing our home.[13]
- We have CD players on each level of our home to play worship music.
- We make a commitment to each other that when one of us awakens in the night, for whatever reason, he or she will use that time to cover the family with prayer. It's amazing how many battles we face in the night watches!
- Lisa and I seek the Lord together for specific Scriptures to pray over each other and each child. As the Holy Spirit emphasizes words from Scripture, we write them out on three-by-five-inch cards, laminate them, and place them on a ring to carry with us. They are great reminders to pray throughout the day for each other. The Lord is so faithful to His Word!

We wouldn't hesitate to protect our homes from an intruder. Likewise, it is critical to the well-being of our families for us men to defend our wives and children in the spiritual realm through prayer. To maximize our effectiveness, we must *believe* that our intercession truly releases God's protective strength over our homes.

Men, seek God for a plan that works for you and your family as you build a peaceful home. The Enemy has a strategy with your name on it, but choose to stand behind the name of the Lord Most

High! We will fight the good fight, and it is our destiny to win. As Winston Churchill said, "We are going to make war and persevere in making war."[14] Churchill found his destiny in the center of the battle. This is where we must stand with our wives and for our children. Tranquility will then reign within our borders.

THE LEGACY OF A PRAYING FATHER

Steve Shanklin

A s strange as it may sound, I had a vision when I was twelve years old that I would one day have two boys. Of course, my mother didn't want to hear her preteen son talking about having children! She sternly advised me to stop thinking about it and keep my mind on school. But I knew God had shown me that my sons would be great men for His kingdom. Sixteen years later, I was the proud father of twin boys! But I have to tell you, they entered this world amid a lot of turbulence.

My wife, Denise, had serious complications with the pregnancy. So I began to pray intensely. She was bedridden for a month before the delivery. The doctor discovered that one of the boys was hemorrhaging inside the womb. I quoted the Bible over them. I clung to verses like Deuteronomy 28:11: "The LORD will grant you abundant prosperity—in the fruit of your womb." While Denise lay helplessly in bed, I knelt beside her and prayed God's Word over her weary body. I knew the situation was serious, but I was clueless that in just a few weeks I would be battling in prayer for the very lives of my wife and boys.

The babies arrived three months early, and things didn't look good. The doctor gave Denise and the boys only a 40 percent chance of survival. Everything I heard pointed to the grim fact that I was about to see my precious wife and sons die. Many of our friends and family were saying that I might lose them. But I went to God. As I held those fragile babies in my hands, I knew I was looking at the fulfillment of a promise the Lord had spoken to a twelve-year-old boy. Their tiny bodies were the same diameter as a Coke can. It took them six months to reach five pounds. God brought us through that traumatic season, and I believe it was the direct result of warring in prayer. The Scriptures anchored my soul and helped to anchor those around me.

Denise had shriveled to eighty-seven pounds. She was gradually restored to health but was still too ill to care for the twins when we brought them home from the hospital at eight months. I remember times during the night when the monitor alarm would go off. I would jump out of bed to find that one of the boys had stopped breathing. I had to shake the little guy to start him breathing again. Talk about a major prayer concern! I spent that season of my life praying without ceasing. I had to take off work for three months to do it, but I dedicated myself to praying over and caring for my family.

I gave my sons the biblical names Christian and Gabriel to remind them of their destiny and the call God has on their lives. Today the boys are fifteen, on fire for God, and very healthy. In the midst of the battle when they were babies, God was telling me, "Steve, you're going to have to fight for your family. You've been talking about prayer, you were raised up in prayer all your life, but now here's a battle for you." God used that year to develop my prayer life. I was unaware that years down the road I would become a national prayer director for Promise Keepers and would write and teach on prayer.

Dads of Prayer

I ONCE HAD the honor of speaking at a conference on prayer with Evelyn Christenson, a true mother in the faith. I mentioned to her how her book *What Happens When Women Pray* was making a significant impact throughout the nation. Then I said, "Evelyn, I *know* what happens when women pray; I have discovered the answer."

With great anticipation, she said, "Steve, tell me!" I think she was expecting my answer to be profound. But I simply said, "When women begin to pray, it automatically causes men to want to know God through prayer. Then they become God's strong watchmen." She smiled and said, "That's the very best result of all, to see men surrender to almighty God in prayer!"

The growing men's prayer movement can be traced back to praying grandmothers, mothers, and wives. Ministries like Evelyn's, Aglow International, Lydia Fellowship, Moms in Touch, and many others have been praying for years that men would take the leadership in prayer for the protection of their families. The spiritual foundation men are standing on today was laid by these precious mothers and handmaidens praying, crying, and calling forth men to be prayer warriors.

It's time for men to step up and take our share of the church's responsibility to pray! One battleground where men's fervent, effectual prayers make a tremendous difference is their children. Our prayers for their destiny, for their protection, and for their future families will reap tremendous fruit. But I've noticed something: my prayer doesn't affect only immediate problems and future situations; it changes me. When I am consistently praying for my children, I am more loving. When I put prayer on the back burner, I tend to grow impatient with them in everyday situations. So praying for my children actually affects my attitude toward them. I've concluded that it is easier to obey the following verse when I'm daily in prayer: "Fathers, don't exasperate your children by coming down hard on them. Take them by the hand and lead them in the way of the Master" (Ephesians 6:4, MSG). Some fathers fail to consistently pray for their children, not because they lack the desire, but because they lack a plan. To find a plan that works for you, stay with me just a little longer.

Prayer Possibilities

I am going to give you three models for praying for your children. I urge you to follow one of these or else to design your own strategy. I have found that if you do not have a simple plan or routine, you will go through cycles of being motivated one day and then slipping into neglect the next. If you have to think up a new approach each day, you will not be able to sustain a consistent prayer covering for your children.

The Bible promise model. The first model is made up of easy-to-apply insights from Cheri Fuller:

> The Bible contains promises concerning His plans for your children, the provision He has available, and what He has in store for them. . . . Look throughout Scripture to see what God desires for young men and women, and let this shape your prayers. For example—
>
> How He wants them to be "taught of the Lord" and how great will be their (and our) peace! (Isaiah 54:13)
>
> How He wants them to hide His Word in their hearts, so they won't sin against Him (Psalm 119:11)
>
> How He wants to fill them with the knowledge of His will (Colossians 1:9)
>
> How He desires that they not lean on their own understanding but trust Him in all their ways (Proverbs 3:5-6)
>
> If you're having difficulty finding appropriate passages, ask God to show you a verse to pray for your child's specific problems.[1]

The Luke 2:52 model. Dick Eastman developed another simple plan.[2] His fourfold pattern for praying for children is based on Luke 2:52, where we see that, as a child, Jesus "grew in wisdom and stature, and in favor with God and men."

First, Luke wrote that Jesus grew in *wisdom.* This prayer focus includes our children's intellectual development, but it encompasses much more than just being smart. Wisdom comes from fearing the Lord (see Psalm 111:10). We need to pray for our children to have a healthy reverence for God, which I define as taking Him and His Word seriously. To grow in wisdom means to increase in knowing the ways of the Lord and reverently obeying them. Someone has defined wisdom as viewing life from God's perspective. What a blessing for children to look at life through God's eyes!

Second, we read that Jesus grew in *stature.* Growing in stature implies healthy physical development. By consistently praying over our children's physical well-being, we are raising a shield of protection over their bodies. Included in this prayer target is the idea of proper care, maintenance, and nutrition for their bodies as well as protection from physical harm and accidents.

Third, the Bible says Jesus increased in *favor with God*. This refers to His relationship with His Father. I want to see my children on fire for God. I want them to have God's favor on what they do. I want them to believe in Him for themselves, not just because they live in a Christian home. May they be able to say to us parents, "Now we believe because we have heard him [Jesus] ourselves, not just because of what you told us. He is indeed the Savior of the world" (John 4:42, NLT). I also like to pray for my offspring to be "strong in spirit" (Luke 1:80, NLT).

The fourth prayer focus is for our children to grow in *favor with men*. Eastman interprets this to include their social development:

I prayed for [my] girls' *social growth*. When the Bible tells us Jesus increased in favor with men, it meant He had gained the respect of those about Him. . . . I prayed that God would give our children good balance in their social relationships. I also prayed for the friends our daughters would select, and for the girls' ability to discern unhealthy friendships.[3]

I would also pray for favor with their teachers and others who play a role in the fulfillment of their destinies (counselors, bosses, future in-laws, and so on).

The bookend model. A third strategy is one that can quickly become a daily tradition that your children will never forget. You can bookend their day with prayer.[4] This approach can help to keep prayer exciting, fresh, and relevant.

Speak a thirty-second prayer or blessing over the kids and give them a hug as they rush off to catch the school bus. It communicates that both God and Dad care about the coming events of their day, and it poises them to tackle it with confidence and faith.

Bedtime prayers lend the perfect opportunity to review the day, thank God for His help, and share about any new needs. Then you can tuck your child in for a peaceful sleep, with all his concerns safe in Jesus' care. Joe White took a verse in Deuteronomy 6 literally: "Impress them [God's commandments] on your children. Talk about them . . . when you lie down and when you get up" (verse 7). He set the goal of spending time with his young children every morning and every night. This is a helpful hint for us dads. He recalls, "When kids are tired at the end of a long day, their defenses are down and they're receptive. They become open and vulnerable at bedtime. . . . Use those times to pray together, read Bible passages, memorize verses, and talk about life."[5] Occasionally you'll hear of a teenager who's reluctant to give up a routine like this. Usually, though, teens want their privacy. But that doesn't mean they want Dad to quit praying!

Richard Foster described bookend prayer this way:

> Try "blessing prayers" as the kids run out the door and "thank-you prayers" as they return. Before the teen years it is especially appropriate to pray over them at night . . . before they go to sleep and again after they are asleep. We can pray for the healing of any emotional traumas from the day, and always we pray prayers of protection.[6]

Praying for our kids does not have to be complicated, but it does need to be consistent. Men, our kids seriously need our prayers. Jesus declared of a character in one of His stories, "While his men were sleeping, his enemy came and sowed tares [weeds] among the wheat" (Matthew 13:25, NASB). Because men have often been spiritually asleep, Satan has stealthily sowed his seeds of destruction in our nation's children. When we awaken and take our place in authoritative prayer, we can actually be a part of changing the spiritual climate over our families and communities.

Prayer Mentoring

An old expression states, "Prayer isn't taught; it's caught." In addition to praying for our children, we are to be prayer mentors. When children see their fathers praying, they can catch that same spirit. I teach my kids to pray not just to get something from God but to get God Himself. When the answers to your prayers are slow in coming, let your kids see you still seeking Him. They will start to understand that prayer is first and foremost a way of relating to the Lord. When you receive an answer to prayer, don't let the opportunity to thank God slip by. This helps to keep prayer alive in your home: "A father tells his sons about Your faithfulness" (Isaiah 38:19, NASB). Children can learn of God's faithfulness through their father's testimonies of His trustworthy care.

Recently, to further mentor my sons, I devised a prayer project. I polled them about what they wanted to accomplish this semester in the school year. They responded: to get good grades, to focus better in class, to be a better witness, to improve their golf game, and so forth. I reminded them that God wants to hear from us (see Jeremiah 33:3). I also explained to them how God is interested in the everyday aspects of their lives (see Philippians 4:6). Instilling the concept of involving the Lord in our daily activities inspired my boys to pray regularly. Consequently, they have a strong prayer life. They challenge me to pray! Now they even initiate prayer with the family.

Finally, to mentor children in prayer, let them see you pray in good times and bad times. One of the greatest things kids can see is how we weather difficult situations. How do we put God's Word into practice in our home? Model a life of devotion through prayer. Those little eyes are watching you. Don't spend too much time teaching them about prayer. We learn to pray by praying. It's never too late to start.

From Generation to Generation

DURING A PROMISE KEEPERS men's conference in Denver in 1995, I was in Mile High Stadium with fifty thousand other men worshiping God. Little did I know that this conference would become a defining moment in my life. Toward the end of the program, the speaker asked all of the young people who had come with their fathers to come down front if they wanted to surrender their lives to serve God and to make a difference in their schools.

Teenage boys began to run from every part of the stadium. Kids were coming from the north, the south, the east, and the west sections of the stadium. Some were running, some were climbing over the rails, but all of them were answering the call with great expectancy and passion. There were around eighteen hundred kids who, in front of their dads and everybody, responded to God's call to dedicate themselves to Him. I had never seen anything like this before.

I immediately began to think of this future generation of young people. I said to myself, *Could one of these young men be the next Moses, Jeremiah, apostle Paul, or John Wesley?* Seeing all the fathers and sons consecrating themselves to God reminded me of this promise:

> The counsel of the LORD stands forever,
>   The plans of His heart from generation to generation.
> (Psalm 33:11, NASB)

I was actually witnessing a fulfillment of this verse—one generation linking God's purposes with the next generation!

To keep this momentum going, we must not depend on large stadium experiences. Men, we will need to build an atmosphere of devotion in our homes.

House of Devotion

I strongly believe that if we keep on doing what we've always done, we'll keep on getting what we've always got. We have to be intentional about making our "Christian homes" really Christian. Here are some simple guidelines I've seen work for my family:

- Regularly take Communion as a family and let this be a time of confessing sins and healing broken relationships. It's a practical way to reinforce this promise: God "will turn the hearts of the fathers to their children, and the hearts of the children to their fathers" (Malachi 4:6).
- Establish a family night. We call our time the "family altar." Every Thursday we meet. Even if I am traveling, we do it by phone. It's a devotional time of prayer and Bible reading. I am letting the kids know that we want to honor God and His Word in our home. I find out their needs, bless them, and ask what the need is for that day. They have a ton of issues going on inside of them. So my wife and I spend time getting them to open up. The key is not so much the length of time we take but the consistency that demonstrates to our kids that we're involved in their lives.
- Memorize Bible verses. I heard one man say that he is paying his children to memorize verses. That's money well spent. Whatever works! One of the best ways to shape our children

from the inside out is to let the Word of God dwell in their hearts and minds. The Bible will also build their faith and give them a strong foundation for prayer.

- Give your children a weekly blessing. Simply place your hands on them and express some reason you are proud of them. Speak a Bible verse over them and then remind them that God has a call and a purpose for their lives. Close with a prayer. I recommend Randy and Lisa Wilson's book *Celebrations of Faith* for more details on blessing your children.[7]
- Fill your homes with godly music and don't allow any evil to invade the home through inappropriate videos, TV, music, and so forth. A friend of mine made a sign to put on top of his TV that says, "I will set no worthless thing before my eyes" (Psalm 101:3, NASB). That's a good reminder!

It is our responsibility, men, to cultivate an awareness of God's presence in our home. The Lord will give you creative ideas to let your children know His reality. All we have to do is ask.

Men of Integrity

As a father, I have tremendous influence over the well-being of my children. I have to take personal responsibility for raising my sons to love and to fear God. It is my job. It is my most significant challenge. It is a battle I must fight and win. My legacy as a father hangs in the balance!

I want my boys to be outstanding men of God. Satan has other ideas. Working through the world's system, he wants my boys to be impure, rebellious, selfish, and living only for the next party. He wants them to despise their father. With immeasurable help from my wife, I have the responsibility to war in prayer for their purity. This is done through prayer, yes, but also by modeling the right way to live. In fact,

> A righteous man who walks in his integrity—
> How blessed are his sons after him. (Proverbs 20:7, NASB)

A covering of peace and grace reaches to our children when we walk in purity and integrity. The reverse is also true. Just as our right living closes the door for sin to reign in our home, so we have the ability to open the door for sin to flourish. Before we go any further, I feel that I need to talk straight with some of you men. Our secret sins have a way of surfacing in our children. Men, if you are worried about your boys looking at pornography on the Internet, my question to you is, have you opened the door by your own impure thoughts?

Being a man of integrity means watching over your words. If you are praying for your child's well-being and future, don't dampen your prayers' effectiveness by speaking destructive words to them: "The tongue has the power of life and death" (Proverbs 18:21). Joyce Meyer elaborated on this verse:

> Our words . . . have a tremendous impact on . . . the lives of others. . . . This is why it is so important that you and I learn to use our words for blessing . . . and building up and not for cursing, wounding, and tearing down. . . . We corrected [our children], but we were careful not to reject them. . . . Say these words . . . and then think about how they make you feel: ugly, stupid, failure, incompetent, slow, clumsy, hopeless. . . . Now speak these words: attractive, intelligent, . . . blessed, creative, talented. . . . I'm sure these words affect you in a much more positive way. . . . Every word we speak can be a brick to build with or a bulldozer to destroy.[8]

Let's be men who choose to build our children's futures.

Leaving a Legacy of Answered Prayer

A MAJOR CHALLENGE in our society is to define the role of men. But God has already defined our role, men. He calls us watchmen — those who will war in prayer for our families, our churches, our communities, and the next generation of warriors.

In 2001 I attended a life-changing rally in Columbus, Ohio. The thrust was to help teenagers move from boyhood to manhood. Like the conference in Denver in 1995, here young men were passionately wanting God to reign in their lives. It deeply impacted me to see these youth kneeling and dedicating themselves to go back into their schools as young warriors on fire for God. I'd never seen that many young people with tears in their eyes. It was real. It was vibrant and intense. It was a God moment. He arrested the lives of teenage boys to become men of God. They caught a spirit of faith and prayer!

As I gazed across the crowd, God was challenging me, "What's going to happen to *your* sons? Will they follow Me? Will they be men that serve Me?"

I said, "Unless You give me the ability to train them to pray, unless You help me to model a life of prayer and faith, I don't know what will happen to them."

When I returned from Columbus, God kept speaking to me, "What about your sons?" With renewed zeal and hope, I decided right then to dedicate myself to influence my boys and thousands of others to make a difference through a life of prayer.

I'm seeing encouraging signs. This is a unique hour in which God is challenging men to cover their families in prayer. Thousands of men are stepping up to answer this call to be men of God. They want their lives to count. A shift is taking place. Dads are beginning to view their children—not money—as their most valuable inheritance and investment. We can direct our kids and release them to make an impact in the world, whether through the church, through business, through science, through education, or through whatever other field they may choose.

My question to you watchmen is, how many times has something problematic or tragic occurred in your family life that could have been prevented? I'm sure that you can say with me that the Lord was faithful to warn you. However, we often don't receive the warning because we have not remained alert. Remember, the trumpet that sounds the alarm to the watchmen will not always awaken those who are asleep. When God is trying to wake us up, we've got to stop hitting the snooze alarm!

Maybe you've dropped the ball regarding your children. Many of us dads have lost some time because we were MIA fathers. We've not been at home. The pursuit of our careers has consumed us. But we can experience a unique aspect of His grace if we'll just show up and say, "God, here I am. Send me. Teach me, so I will be able to lead my children in Your ways. Make up for the time that was lost in previous years. Make a difference in the lives of my children and grandkids through prayer and Your Word." If men will just begin to say "Yes,

Lord," God promises that He will show them how to make it happen.

My challenge to you is to answer God's call. He is looking for men of faith, men of the Word, men of prayer, men to influence the next generation. Our homes can be turned around when we take the time to pray for and bless our kids. If you haven't been covering your children in prayer, make a change. I urge you to say, "I'll start today to pray over my kids at home and as I drive to work. I'll speak the Word of God over them." It will make all the difference in the world.

O. Hallesby counseled men nearly half a century ago: "My friend, if you are not able to leave your children a legacy in the form of goods, do not worry about that . . . but see to it, night and day, that you pray for them. Then you will leave them a great legacy of answers to prayer, which will follow them all the days of their life."[9]

KINGDOMS CLASHING KINGDOMS CLASHING KINGDOMS CLASHING KINGDOMS CLASHING
KINGDOMS CLASHING KINGDOMS CLASHING KINGDOMS CLASHING KINGDOMS CLASHING
KINGDOMS CLASHING KINGDOMS CLASHING KINGDOMS CLASHING KINGDOMS CLASHING
KINGDOMS CLASHING KINGDOMS CLASHING KINGDOMS CLASHING KINGDOMS CLASHING
KINGDOMS CLASHING KINGDOMS CLASHING KINGDOMS CLASHING KINGDOMS CLASHING
KINGDOMS CLASHING KINGDOMS CLASHING KINGDOMS CLASHING KINGDOMS CLASHING
KINGDOMS CLASHING KINGDOMS CLASHING KINGDOMS CLASHING KINGDOMS CLASHING
KINGDOMS CLASHING KINGDOMS CLASHING KINGDOMS CLASHING KINGDOMS CLASHING
KINGDOMS CLASHING KINGDOMS CLASHING KINGDOMS CLASHING KINGDOMS CLASHING
KINGDOMS CLASHING KINGDOMS CLASHING KINGDOMS CLASHING KINGDOMS CLASHING
KINGDOMS CLASHING KINGDOMS CLASHING KINGDOMS CLASHING KINGDOMS CLASHING
KINGDOMS CLASHING KINGDOMS CLASHING KINGDOMS CLASHING KINGDOMS CLASHING
KINGDOMS CLASHING KINGDOMS CLASHING KINGDOMS CLASHING KINGDOMS CLASHING
KINGDOMS CLASHING KINGDOMS CLASHING KINGDOMS CLASHING KINGDOMS CLASHING

Part 3

KINGDOMS CLASHING

LIFESTYLE WARFARE

Ted Haggard

When I was growing up in Delphi, Indiana, many of the store owners didn't lock their doors at night because they thought someone might need something. I remember my dad and I went into the ACE Hardware store late one night and picked up a rake. My dad left the money to pay for it and a thank-you note on the cash register telling the owner that he had taken the rake. Think of that. Now I'm forty-five years old and live in Colorado Springs, Colorado, one of the safest cities in America. But we would never think of doing that. Why? Because the moral climate of our communities has drastically changed.

Why is our nation in this shape? Part of the reason is because we are seeing an integrity crisis within the church. Let's face it: the church, as a whole, has not modeled exemplary behavior. Consequently, we haven't significantly impacted society and influenced our cities for God. The best way for the church to see a change in the community is by believers building strong families, living godly lives, treating others right, and praying for hearts to be open to the gospel.

In my mind, what validates the importance of prayer in a man's experience is the overall effectiveness it adds to his life. My first models of born-again Christians were men committed to prayer. During my high school years, I went to a church where the pastor had a vibrant prayer life. I attended a Christian university, and my professors emphasized the power of prayer. My first experience on the mission field taught me that successful missionaries were prayerful missionaries. Because I admired my pastor, my professors, and the missionaries I had met, I sensed that prayer was linked to something in the core of a man to make him stable, honorable, and wise. As I grow older, it's becoming clear to me that godly people don't just pray in their prayer closets; they also communicate their love to God through their lifestyles. No doubt, the way they pay their bills, connect with their families, and treat others in the community is as much a part of their prayer lives as are the words they say to God in private.

Because of my experience, it rarely occurs to me that there are Christian men who don't pray. Imagine that! Why wouldn't believing men want to pray? Why wouldn't we want to have more of God's strength and power in our lives? Why wouldn't we want to bless those around us? I've heard that some men think of prayer as something that women ought to do, but that just doesn't make sense to me. Throughout the history of Christianity, courageous men of God who have impacted their society have been men of prayer. Where did Martin Luther find boldness to confront a corrupt church? Prayer. How did that other Martin Luther (King, Jr.) gain strength to break the chains of bigotry? Prayer.

Prayer Is Not an Escape
We are all commissioned to "pray without ceasing" (1 Thessalonians 5:17, NASB). But how? If you view prayer as an isolated activity, praying without ceasing is impossible. The key is to not separate our prayer lives from the way we live. "Prayer is not escape from reality," William Barclay wrote. "Prayer is not [simply] secluded meditation . . . with God. Prayer and action go hand in hand."[1]

This came alive to me one day after I returned from a long trip. I had left the hotel for the airport early that morning, so I didn't take the time to read my Bible and pray, which is my normal routine. When I arrived home, my wife and children were in the back yard playing ball. I greeted them and played for a short while but felt guilty about not spending time with the Lord that morning. So I excused myself and went into the house to pray. When I started praying, I sensed the conviction of the Holy Spirit in my heart. I felt the Lord pointing out that in prayer I commune with Him and resist the powers of darkness for myself, my family, and others. But today He was showing me that if I would play ball with my kids, it would also achieve spiritual results. They had missed me; they needed me. Basically, He was saying to me, "Play now; pray later."

I saw it. I got the principle. By demonstrating to my family that I love them, I'm communicating to God that I honor Him. This idea raced through my mind: by showing respect to others, maintaining integrity, serving them, and learning the art of long-lasting, healthy relationships, prayer can have its greatest effect through my life. I'm not saying our actions can take the place of private prayer. Never. I am saying our lives are inseparable from our prayers. No, I think I want to say it stronger than that. If our verbal prayers and our lifestyle contradict one another, our lifestyle tells the real story. There. That's it! The essence of prayer isn't merely folding your hands, getting on your knees, closing your eyes, or speaking out loud. It's receiving the power to impact your family and community after spending time in God's presence. Prayer first changes my life, then it influences the lives around me.

The Power of Prayer to Change Me

THE PRIMARY PURPOSE of prayer is for us to get to know our heavenly Father better. Next, we pray in order to receive the power of God to live the kind of life He has for us. Most mornings when I get up, the first thing I do is go into a private room for an hour to pray and read my Bible. I do it because I know that every day holds situations that will be opportunities either for great success or for great difficulty. I want to win. So let me share some ways I let prayer change me.

Power Over My Old Sin Nature
Okay, gentlemen, let's talk shop. Every one of us has an old sin nature that wants to ruin our lives. You know the routine: that "old man" on the inside whom we hate but who shows up at the most inopportune times! This is the reason pastors fail, people leave churches in a huff, and guys go after new wives. It is the dark impulse that makes men

treat their children badly, steal from their bosses, and say the wrong things to the wrong people at the wrong time. It is ruthless and tireless and will stop at nothing to drag us down. It must die!

The apostle Paul made an amazing declaration: "I die every day—I mean that, brothers" (1 Corinthians 15:31). He further explained, "I *have been crucified* with Christ and I *no longer live,* but Christ lives in me. The life I live in the body, I live by faith in the Son of God, who loved me and gave himself for me" (Galatians 2:20, emphasis added). Notice he was saying our old sinful nature has been crucified. That's past tense! Christ dealt it a death blow on the cross. We must daily ask God to make this real in our lives, or we won't experience the victory that comes with this truth. Paul knew that the only way to live successful, clean, honorable Christian lives is to let Christ's power kill our worst desires every day. Violently. Strategically. With force. We have to be more ruthless against our sinful nature than our sinful nature is against us.

In prayer, you can talk to God about your worst thoughts and deal with your darkest desires. You can confront them, see them plainly, and tell yourself that they are defeated and dead by the power of Christ's cross.

The bottom line is that you will either be full of the Spirit or full of sin. The choice is yours. You can either enjoy the fruit and power of the Holy Spirit or live under the tyranny of the sinful nature. If you want to take the chance of losing your family and your integrity, then watch TV until late at night and sleep too late in the mornings to pray. But if you want to live a life of joy and power, then you have to daily come to God in faith and let Him give you the power from Christ's work on the cross to conquer your old nature.

The Power of God's Word

During my morning prayer times, I like to read four chapters of the Bible. I read one chapter from the Old Testament, one from the New, one from Psalms, and one from Proverbs. This keeps me refreshed in God's Word. In addition, I have memorized many key passages in the Bible that are helpful in prayer. For example, I often pray through the fruit of the Spirit: "love, joy, peace, patience, kindness, goodness, faithfulness, gentleness and self-control. Against such things there is no law" (Galatians 5:22-23). These verses often come to mind when I'm tempted to become impatient or to be unkind in some situation. Praying through the fruit of the Spirit from memory integrates these qualities into my life so that my day-to-day attitude is noticeably improved.

Think of the marriages saved, the businesses restored, the relationships healed simply by men praying God's Word and allowing the Holy Spirit to work these characteristics into their lives. But if we fail to pray, our sinful natures will dominate our lives and the fruit of the Spirit will not be evident. So we've got to get up, beat back our sinfulness, be filled with God's Word, and pray for the fruit of the Holy Spirit.

Power to Practice Love and Kindness

Prayer doesn't stop when we leave our morning devotions. In fact, our prayers for the day are just beginning. Because we live in a love-starved world, I've found that when I leave my morning prayer time, I just about always come across a situation in which people need love and kindness in order to make their day work. I frequently ask God to fill me with His heart of love and compassion.

Recently, I received a phone call from a distraught mother who was concerned for her teenage son and some of the friends he was making. Because of this mother's distress, she was irrational and rude. If my sinful nature had been in charge of my life that day, I might have reacted to her forcefulness and persistence. But she didn't need that. She needed me to listen, to be patient, and to be kind. I can only do that with the power that comes from my morning devotions.

Power to Walk in Humility and Forgiveness

When we walk in humility and forgiveness, we may go through the same situations that leave others hurt, angry, bitter, and sometimes vengeful. Yet we don't have to respond negatively if we maintain a position of humility with others and are quick to forgive.

Each winter, spring, summer, and fall, I take three days and go somewhere alone to pray and fast. During these times, I always ask God to bring to my mind everyone whom I need to forgive. One time I found myself taking two of the three days forgiving others. Wow! And I hadn't even known that my heart was slowly getting hard. But it was. Those two days of forgiving others, followed by a third day of praying in great freedom, set me up for a strong season of life afterward.

Prayer times are extremely valuable. They give us the power to love our wife and kids and live a clean life. It's here that we fill our heart and mind with God's Word, receive power to practice love and kindness, and find grace to be humble and forgiving. These are the best ways to live a successful life.

Praying from an Offensive Position

WHEN WE PRAY, we are changed. Then one of the benefits we receive is greater positive influence in the lives of those around us. It's incredible, but our character can be a deciding factor in somebody else's salvation. When you pray for others who know Christ, you are making a great difference in their lives. Your prayers help them to receive God's strength, grace, wisdom, and protection. When you pray for those who do not know Christ, you are stimulating the ministry of the Holy Spirit around them and are thwarting the deceiving influences of darkness. This gives them a greater opportunity to respond positively to the message of the gospel.

Remember that you do not have the authority to change people's minds, but you do have the authority to influence the spiritual activity around them through prayer. Also, keep in mind, when we are praying for unbelievers to come to Christ, we are to pray from an offensive position. Guys, I'm going to give you a little theology lesson on spiritual warfare. If you hear what these five men are saying, it will revolutionize your approach to the Christian life.

Chuck Kraft and Mark White described how all this mess with Satan began: Through Adam's disobedience (Genesis 3), Satan received dominion over the earth, and thus humankind surrendered their original authority (Genesis 1:28). Satan, having been cast out of heaven (see Isaiah 14:13-14), usurped control over the earth through deceit.[2]

Peter Wagner defined our Enemy's key tasks in a nutshell: "Satan's central task and desire is to prevent God from being glorified . . . by keeping lost people from being saved. . . . Satan's secondary objective is to make human beings and human society as miserable as possible in this present life."[3]

James Kallas wrote, "A war is going on! Cosmic war! Jesus is the divine invader sent by God to shatter the strengths of Satan."[4] That means that we are the invaders on the offensive and that Satan and his kingdom are placed in a defensive posture (see Matthew 11:12). Most men think just the opposite!

John Wimber boiled it down to this:

> Who is attacking the territory of the other, Christ or Satan, and what difference does the answer to this question make to Christians? The difference affects our attitude and stance toward the Christian life. If Jesus is the invader, Satan is consigned to the defensive. We become offensive soldiers, taking territory and redeeming lives.[5]

Spheres of Influence

NOW, MEN, LET'S go on the offensive in our spheres of influence. But first, read this closely: "The LORD God took the man and put him in the Garden of Eden to work it and take care of it" (Genesis 2:15). Here is the good news, guys. We were created to work. We were created to care for our Eden. In order for every one of us to understand our fundamental purpose in being created, we have to determine what our Eden is and how we are supposed to care for it.

I believe that all of us have four primary spheres of influence or Gardens of Eden: our homes, our churches, our communities, and our places of work. We are responsible to care for and work in each of these areas. But first we must pray. We need to ask God to reveal to us the real battlefronts in each of these "gardens." For example, when unbelievers are in our spheres of influence, we need to be able to pray with intensity and passion. This passion springs from an understanding of the reality of heaven and the reality of hell, the finality of heaven and the finality of hell, and the joy of heaven and the needless suffering of hell. I want to make it difficult for anyone in my gardens to go to hell. So how can I do that?

Your prayers can make the difference, as the apostle Paul instructed: "We are human, but we don't wage war with human plans and methods. We use God's mighty weapons, not mere worldly weapons, to knock down the Devil's strongholds. With these weapons we break down every proud argument *that keeps people from knowing God*" (2 Corinthians 10:3-5, NLT, emphasis added). Yes, your prayers over people who do not follow Christ can make a difference.

Armed with these insights, let's look at each garden individually.

Home

When I pray in the morning, the first thing I pray for is my home. I know that God created me to care for my home, and that knowledge motivates me to pray for my wife, my children, and my children's future spouses. As I pray for them, I can see, in my heart, the Spirit of God giving them favor, wisdom, insight, knowledge, and protection as they go through their day. My children face the same things every other child faces, but it feels different to them because they have a dad who loves them so much that he prays for them every day.

Living an honorable life is one of the secrets to making a home work. When my children know that they can trust my word, my provision, and my judgment, then we don't face nearly the number of difficult situations that some families face. A friend of mine was telling me how much he loved his dad, so I asked him why. He said, "I've never seen my dad look at another woman or heard him tell a lie. He's a great man. I want to be just like him." That story says it all for me! Now suppose that father had unbelieving children. His life of integrity would help soften their hearts to one day receive the gospel. It's crucial to remember, though, that "Satan . . . has blinded the minds of those who don't believe, so they are unable to see. . . . They don't understand the message . . . of Christ" (2 Corinthians 4:4, NLT). So, in addition to being a good living example of Christianity, the father should pray that the spiritual blindfolds would be removed and the children would open their hearts to God's love.

Church

After praying for my home, I pray for the local church where I am raising my family. The local church can be a virtually unlimited source of blessing, love, security, and support. But if things go awry, a church can be as hurtful as a dysfunctional family. The surest way to protect our churches is to faithfully pray for the members. If churches are prayed for, they can avoid the pitfalls that harm so many believers. Everyone's lives are strengthened by a faithful, growing local church. So it's well worth my time to bless my church every day. I smile as I pray blessings over the pastors, staff, elders, trustees, small-group leaders, volunteers, and other members. I know as I pray for them that their strength is a blessing to my family and our entire community.

In the church I pastor, we have more than eight hundred small groups, the majority of which are led by men who are discipling others in every subject imaginable. When a healthy church is mobilizing ministry throughout the community, then it makes it much easier for those who don't know the Lord to respond positively to Him. I pray for the church to be filled with people who have a heart to share Christ's message of eternal life in their spheres of influence. When that happens, it can be as in the first Christian church. They enjoyed "the favor of all the people. And the Lord added to their number daily those who were being saved" (Acts 2:47).

Community

I pray for the governmental leaders in my city, state, and nation who come to mind. I also cover my neighborhood and community in prayer regularly. I pray for schools and homes and police officers and neighborhoods and families. I pray that the people of my community will be protected, that they will prosper, and that they will know salvation through Jesus Christ. When I drive through my neighborhood, I try not to look at buildings and houses as mere physical structures, but rather I focus my prayers on the humans living there. I ask God to use me to reveal His love to them, because "the righteous is a guide to his neighbor" (Proverbs 12:26, NASB). If I am a righteous man in Christ, then the Lord expects me to influence my neighbors in the truth.

Workplace

Finally, I pray for my own place of work. I cover in prayer those whom I work for and those who work for me and those who receive the services that we provide as a team. No matter what you do for a living, it is vital to pray for your job, for those who work with you, and for those you serve. As we pray, we can trust the Lord to increase efficiency, produce prosperity, and diminish the stress of the work environment. If you know fellow believers in your workplace, try to gather for a few minutes daily or weekly to pray. I have heard many stories of two or three men meeting at their workplace for prayer and God beginning to change the lives of their coworkers. Some who had walked away from the Lord returned with renewed dedication. Some who didn't know Christ surrendered their lives to Him. Your prayers can truly change the spiritual climate where you work!

Your Life Can Make a Difference

LIVING THE GOSPEL is spiritual warfare. Hugging your kids and playing a board game with them opens their hearts to God and helps to block the powers of darkness from their lives. A godly life is a powerful weapon to oppose the Enemy. Of course, the opposite is also true. You can have your prayer time, but if you get up off your knees still resenting your wife and feeling bitter toward your kids, you will make it difficult for God to touch them, and you might open a door for the powers of darkness to influence them.

So prayer comes down to our relationships. It's in the midst of our relationships that good or evil will surface. Our decisions about what to do when someone owes us money, or when we owe someone money, reveal our hearts. Honest business, the keeping of our word, and the wisdom to handle situations well so others can trust us are the fruit of a strong prayer life.

When people in your community have a positive relationship with you, they will listen to you and have open hearts toward you so that you can impact their lives in a greater way. My dad was a businessman in a small town in Indiana, as I mentioned earlier. At one stage in his career, another businessman in town made some horrible mistakes and lost his reputation and his business. He ended up abandoning his family and leaving the community. His daughter was getting married, and in the midst of her heartbreak over her father's shame, she asked my dad to walk her down the aisle in her wedding. No doubt, my dad was a man of prayer. But his prayer didn't stay in the closet. His prayer life made him an honorable man, which included walking an embarrassed friend's daughter down the aisle. When I saw that, it taught me about God.

So, men, your life reflects your prayers. Andrew Murray put it this way: "It is as men live that they pray. It is the life that prays."[6] Have a great prayer life and be filled with the Holy Spirit every day so that your time with your family and your time in your prayer closet are saying the same thing—that God has done a miracle in you.

SKILLS AND WEAPONS OF WAR

Calvin Johnson

I t was June 1996 when we rushed our son Calvin, Jr., to the hospital with a high fever and excruciating pain. Immediately he was admitted to ICU. The doctor assured us that everything was going to be just fine. But three days later, Calvin's condition worsened. The doctors ran a series of tests that showed he had contracted some type of Mediterranean disease. The bad news was that the medical staff in Colorado didn't know how to treat it. Our little seven-year-old was screaming in agony and crying, "Help me!" Can you imagine how I felt? "Help me! Please, Dad! Help me! I've seen you pray before, and it worked. So how come your prayers aren't working now?"

That hit me like a ton of bricks! Tears filled my eyes. Staggering into the hallway, I fell on my knees and cried out to God in deep desperation like I had never done before. Less than twenty-four hours later, Calvin was released from the hospital and has been healthy ever since. You see, men, extreme circumstances require crying out to God in desperation.

The Cry of Desperation

WE ARE LIVING in a time of escalated spiritual warfare. When you are at the end of your rope, I implore you to cry out for God's intervention, just as I did for my son. Our little now-I-lay-me-down-to-sleep prayers aren't going to change anything. We need to pray with the same intensity with which Jesus prayed. "During the days of Jesus' life on earth, he offered up prayers and petitions with loud cries and tears to the one who could save him" (Hebrews 5:7). Tears do add power to our intercession. I like how Charles Spurgeon described tears as liquid prayers.[1]

The cry of desperation comes from a heart filled with anguish and pain, calling out to God without any inhibition or restraint. It is prayer void of etiquette, religious-sounding verbiage, or politically correct phraseology. It can be defined as relentless prayer that will not give up and will not give in but goes on until the answer comes. It moves our heavenly Father's heart the same way my son's cries moved my heart.

Throughout the Scriptures, we observe many instances in which people cried out to God in desperation and He answered. Two accounts in the gospel of Mark are particularly dramatic. There's the heartrending story of a father who had a demon-possessed son. This dad cried out to Jesus, and the boy was delivered (see 9:14-27). The other account is found in the next chapter. A blind beggar named Bartimaeus fervently yelled out to Jesus to restore his sight (see 10:46-52). The Lord immediately responded, and Bartimaeus lost his job as a blind beggar.

There are times we need to abandon our dignity and pray as if someone's life depended upon it. I now realize that this "cry of desperation" type of praying is actually a spiritual weapon. It's a part of our heavy artillery, and it is effective in times of extreme crisis. I call it a spiritual weapon because it is so forceful that no demon can weaken it. And when God's children cry out in desperation while under a spiritual attack, the Enemy flees in terror. He knows he's been messing with one of God's kids, and now Father is about to show up!

The School of Spiritual Warfare

SOLDIERS KNOW THAT there is no victory in combat without weapons. But they also understand that powerful weaponry must be coupled with great skill, because one without the other spells disaster. Soldiers commit countless hours to rigorous strength conditioning, skill development, and weapons training. Success in battle occurs only because soldiers have placed value on personal preparedness.

Unfortunately, many Christian men today have placed little or no value on being spiritually prepared. This is because they have not understood spiritual warfare. One of my goals as a pastor is to help men develop their God-given warrior skills so they can effectively wield their awesome arsenal of spiritual weaponry.

I remember how, back in 1992, when I started Solid Rock Christian Church, I felt an unbelievable resistance of evil. This was different from any experience I had ever faced. I was ill prepared and unable to pinpoint the appropriate steps to overcome these forces resisting me. Understanding spiritual warfare was not a focus in my black Baptist tradition, so I really had not given it much thought. But I quickly changed my mind when I realized that there were spiritual enemies viciously opposing God's vision for my life and Solid Rock Christian Church.

Bizarre things began to happen. I was almost fired from my job. I had never been disciplined or even reprimanded in thirteen years. Suddenly I was in hot water and didn't know why. Then my pastor, who had blessed my plans to start a church, accused me of trying to undermine his ministry. To make matters worse, someone stole my checkbook and started forging my signature!

Personal, professional, legal, and spiritual challenges popped up so frequently that I found myself struggling daily just to maintain a consistent prayer time. This season marked my introduction to spiritual warfare and, hard as it was, I thank God that He taught me to hone my spiritual weapons and sharpen my prayer skills.

Discernment: A Basic Skill for Spiritual Battles

DISCERNMENT IS ONE skill I believe every Christian man must develop. The ability to discern lays the groundwork for all that we do in spiritual battle. To discern means to recognize and distinguish clearly. We must learn to distinguish whether we are being spiritually attacked, going through a simple faith test, or struggling with fallen human nature. Often we write things off as coincidences, problems with living in an imperfect world, or human reactions, when in essence they are demonic attacks. Please understand, I am not suggesting that there is a demon behind every bad thing that happens to us. But I do believe many negative events have demonic origins, and men must be trained to know the difference. Corrie ten Boom once said, "It's a poor soldier indeed who does not recognize the enemy."[2]

The apostle Paul wrote, "We are not fighting against people made of flesh and blood, but against the evil rulers and authorities of the unseen world, against those mighty powers of darkness who rule this world, and against wicked spirits in the heavenly realms" (Ephesians 6:12, NLT). This verse tells us that we face more than just natural enemies. So, men, how do we know when we are being attacked? Gary Kinnaman gives us these insights:

> Discernment is . . . a learned skill. The writer of Hebrews describes mature Christians as those "who by constant use have trained themselves to distinguish good and evil" (Hebrews 5:14, NASB). Spiritual maturity and wise perception do not develop overnight. There is no getting around it. Sometimes we just have to learn the hard way, chopping a path through the jungle of experience. The only way to get older and wiser is to get older — and wiser![3]

Basically, we learn discernment through trial and error. If you think you may be under spiritual attack, ask the Lord to let you know what to do. He promises to share His infinite wisdom with us (see James 1:5). Our spiritual discernment will be sharpened by our daily spending time in God's Word. One key verse to remember is Proverbs 2:3:

> If you cry for discernment,
>   Lift your voice for understanding. (NASB)

Discernment is only half of what we need. After discerning the source of the battle, we will need understanding of what to do next.

When all your attempts to correct a problem seem to fail, maybe your mistake is in trying to fight a spiritual battle with human weapons, such as hard work and reason. Imagine a man who has been praying daily with his family, discipling them in the Scriptures, and rejoicing in their growth. Then suddenly the family loses interest in spiritual things. Disorder and chaos ensue. The home is filled with heaviness, strife, and oppression. Then the children, who are typically obedient, rebel. Or the wife becomes depressed for no good reason. The man discerns that an unseen enemy is the spiritual source of this chaos and then begins to battle on his knees for his family.

A scenario like this would be a red alert to employ available weaponry and engage the enemy in battle. Simply put, a skilled warrior senses opposition and responds accordingly. But a wise man does not grab just any weapon or fight just any fight. He first evaluates the situation and then devises a battle plan based on his best intelligence reports about the opponent.

If we are to defeat the Devil, we must understand his tactics and capabilities. The following intelligence will never be outdated, because we find it in the Bible. The Devil's character will never change, and these truths will eternally incriminate him.

- He is looking for victims to destroy. "Be careful! Watch out for attacks from the Devil, your great enemy. He prowls around like a roaring lion, looking for some victim to devour" (1 Peter 5:8, NLT).
- He is incapable of telling the truth. "[The Devil] was a murderer from the beginning and has always hated the truth. There is no truth in him. When he lies, it is consistent with his character; for he is a liar and the father of lies" (John 8:44, NLT).
- He is a serpent. "This great dragon—the ancient serpent called the Devil, or Satan, the one deceiving the whole world—was thrown down to the earth with all his angels" (Revelation 12:9, NLT).
- He is the Accuser. "The Accuser has been thrown down to earth—the one who accused our brothers and sisters before our God day and night" (Revelation 12:10, NLT).
- He is a thief who steals the truth of the Word. "The seed that fell on the hard path represents those who hear the message, but then Satan comes at once and takes it away from them" (Mark 4:15, NLT).

Once the intelligence information has been gathered, it's time to ready the weapons. Men, this is one of the most exciting parts of spiritual warfare: discovering the arsenal of weapons God wants us to access. The first time that I learned what an awesome assortment of spiritual weapons the Commander in Chief, Jesus Christ, gave to His church, I shouted! Well, call me stupid, but I never knew that Christians had weapons! This was a major turning point in my life because, up until then, the Devil was beating up on me, my family, and our church at will because I was not using the spiritual weapons of war.

I had read Paul's words—"The weapons we fight with are not the weapons of the world. On the contrary, they have divine power to demolish strongholds" (2 Corinthians 10:4)—but I had never taken the time to find out specifically what those weapons were. When I finally studied spiritual weapons and their proper use, I noticed an increased grace and strength to pray for my church and my family's health and protection.

An Awesome Arsenal

SO NOW YOU can see why I get excited about the Lord's weapons! They have made a tremendous difference in my daily relationship with Christ. Because many books deal with the well-known spiritual armor listed in Ephesians 6:10-18, I will look at some of the other weapons for our use. I have four favorites that I would like to share with you, along with some examples of how to use them in spiritual warfare.

Spirit-filled, Persistent Prayer

Let me begin with my number-one resource: Spirit-filled, persistent prayer. This is Holy Spirit-directed prayer that compels us to pray only the Father's will until it is established. The Bible encourages us to pray this way: "Pray at all times and on every occasion in the power of the Holy Spirit. Stay alert and be persistent in your prayers for all Christians everywhere" (Ephesians 6:18, NLT).

One day Jesus told His disciples a story to illustrate their need for constant prayer and to show them that they must never give up:

> "There was a judge in a certain city," he [Jesus] said, "who was a godless man with great contempt for everyone. A widow of

that city came to him repeatedly, appealing for justice against someone who had harmed her. The judge ignored her for a while, but eventually she wore him out. 'I fear neither God nor man,' he said to himself, 'but this woman is driving me crazy. I'm going to see that she gets justice, because she is wearing me out with her constant requests!'"

Then the Lord said, "Learn a lesson from this evil judge. Even he rendered a just decision in the end, so don't you think God will surely give justice to his chosen people who plead with him day and night? Will he keep putting them off? I tell you, he will grant justice to them quickly!" (Luke 18:2-8, NLT)

I learned how to use the weapon of Spirit-filled, persistent prayer in 1994 when God told me that He would move the church I was pastoring (sixty-five people) into a new facility. Looking at our financial picture, I knew that it would be a miracle if it happened. So I began praying daily, not for finances or for a building, but just for the fulfillment of the promise God had given me. A few months later, I saw God's word fulfilled when the church moved into a brand-new storefront building on one of the main boulevards in our city. Let me tell you, we experienced tremendous opposition, but our key to victory was Spirit-filled, persistent prayer.

So let me encourage you, men, to keep praying daily for the fulfillment of what God has spoken to you, and you will see His promises come to pass. Perhaps your prayers focus on the destiny of your children or the healing of a broken relationship within your family. Keep praying with persistence and don't forget to access the power of the Spirit. The key verses explaining the Holy Spirit's work in our prayers are Romans 8:26 and 27:

The Holy Spirit helps us in our distress. For we don't even know what we should pray for, nor how we should pray. But the Holy Spirit prays for us with groanings that cannot be expressed in words. And the Father who knows all hearts knows what the Spirit is saying, for the Spirit pleads for us believers in harmony with God's own will. (NLT)

If, for example, your teenager is involved with a rough crowd, drugs, immorality, or witchcraft, you, as the father, must stand up and fight for your child. Spirit-filled praying means you are not alone in your praying. The Holy Spirit is here to help us. Here is how Jack Hayford explained Romans 8:26: The Holy Spirit "is active in (1) bringing to mind people or circumstances we ought to pray for, and (2) giving rise to prayer that exactly hits the mark. That is, God Himself knows where hearts cry for His intervention, and the Holy Spirit prompts prayer to release the working of His hand for them."[4]

Let's ask the Holy Spirit to help us in all areas of our lives, especially in our prayers. Richard Foster eloquently summarized the Holy Spirit's support during our praying: "When we stumble over our words, the Spirit straightens out the syntax. When we pray with muddy motives, the Spirit purifies the stream. . . . The point is that we do not have to have everything perfect when we pray. The Spirit reshapes, refines, and reinterprets our feeble, ego-driven prayers."[5]

The Word of God

The second weapon is the Word of God, or the Bible. We must value God's Word because it holds all the answers to our Enemy's temptations and attacks against our minds. The apostle Paul instructed us, "Take the sword of the Spirit, which is the word of God" (Ephesians 6:17, NLT). Hebrews 4:12 tells us how mighty the Word is: "The word of God is living and active. Sharper than any double-edged sword, . . . it judges the thoughts and attitudes of the heart."

Jesus demonstrated this power when He used Scripture to defeat the temptations of the Devil.

> The Devil came and said to him, "If you are the Son of God, change these stones into loaves of bread."
> But Jesus told him, "No! The Scriptures say,
> 'People need more than bread for their life;
> they must feed on every word of God.'"
> Then the Devil took him to Jerusalem, to the highest point of the Temple, and said, "If you are the Son of God, jump off! For the Scriptures say,
> 'He orders his angels to protect you.
> And they will hold you with their hands
> to keep you from striking your foot on a stone.'"

Jesus responded, "The Scriptures also say, 'Do not test the Lord your God.'"

Next the Devil took him to the peak of a very high mountain and showed him the nations of the world and all their glory. "I will give it all to you," he said, "if you will only kneel down and worship me."

"Get out of here, Satan," Jesus told him. "For the Scriptures say,

'You must worship the Lord your God;
serve only him.'"

Then the Devil went away. (Matthew 4:3-11, NLT)

Jesus showed us that, when we are dealing with demonic temptation, we must use the Word to stop these insidious assaults. Notice, when Jesus spoke Scripture, the temptation ended and the Devil finally left. If we want to see victory, then we must place a high value on learning and memorizing God's Word. It has the power to defuse these kinds of attacks.

Suppose you are being tempted to lust. You can quote verses like this one:

Turn away my eyes from looking at vanity,
And revive me in Your ways. (Psalm 119:37, NASB)

The Word of God has power to help you control your thoughts. If you are battling fear, quote the Bible, as Jesus did. God's Word can give the strength you need: "God hath not given us the spirit of fear; but of power, and of love, and of a sound mind" (2 Timothy 1:7, KJV). Next time you sense the Evil One barraging your mind with lust, fear, or any other ungodly thoughts, pick up your sword and fight!

Praise

We see in both the Old and New Testaments that praise is a powerful weapon (see 2 Chronicles 20:20-23; Acts 16:25-28.) Simply stated, praise is boasting in God's person and power. Praise exalts God above our enemies and circumstances. When we praise Him, we are releasing our faith. We are declaring that He is superior to anyone or anything.

Let me tell you what happened when our church members went out to pray through a neighborhood in our city that was plagued with crime, drugs, and violence. We arrived at our destination and began to pray in our usual way. Then one of the men came up to me and said, "Pastor, I believe the Lord is saying we need to sing and praise Him." I agreed, so we called everyone together and explained the plan to them. Then we began to sing "What a Mighty God We Serve." Simple enough, right? After singing, we lifted our voices and exalted God by declaring His awesomeness, power, and splendor.

Two days later, our local newspaper reported that the police had made major drug busts and had helped apartment owners evict suspected criminals right in that neighborhood! God truly inhabits the praises of His people (see Psalm 22:3), and we were able to see His presence come into a spiritually dark place through praise. It certainly is a powerful weapon.

I have had people tell me that a feeling of heaviness sometimes invades their home. Family members fight depression and hopelessness. Brother, praise is the best weapon to fight this negative force. The Bible encourages us to put on a garment of praise in place of the spirit of heaviness (see Isaiah 61:3). Play worship and praise music throughout your home and see how the atmosphere changes. Jack Taylor gives this insight into the power of praise: "Praise, the continuing exercise of heaven, is clearly etched into the memory of the devil and every other fallen angel. . . . When they hear biblical praises they are driven to panic. . . . Their ranks are broken. Like metal scratching glass is the sound of praises to them."[6]

Love

The final weapon I'll mention is the nuclear weapon of love. To truly love someone, we cannot be consumed with ourselves. Sacrificial love overcomes the Devil because it lays down its life for others. It's as the voice from heaven in Revelation says of those who defeat Satan:

> They weren't in love with themselves;
>   they were willing to die for Christ. (12:11, MSG)

Satan cannot manipulate someone who is selflessly living for others.

Love has the power to heal broken hearts, repair breaches in relationships, abolish the evils of racism, and annihilate the sin of humanity while reconciling us to God. Love is all-powerful because God is love (see 1 John 4:16). God demonstrated the strength of this weapon when He gave Jesus, His only Son, to die for the sins of humanity (see John 3:16, Romans 5:6-8). This is a perfect illustration of how much power and impact love delivers: the human race was doomed to die, Satan's weapons of sin and death were in full effect, then God deployed the nuclear weapon of love! Today we can live in victory because love never fails. Love is the most essential weapon of all, because it possesses limitless capabilities.

The deployment of love as a weapon may sound strange, but you must understand that love holds nothing back. In order to grasp the essence of love, consider 1 Corinthians 13:4-7 (NLT):

> Love is patient and kind. Love is not jealous or boastful or proud or rude. Love does not demand its own way. Love is not irritable, and it keeps no record of when it has been wronged. It is never glad about injustice but rejoices whenever truth wins out. Love never gives up, never loses faith, is always hopeful, and endures through every circumstance.

Men, if you want your marriage to succeed, you have to use this biblical weapon of love. If you want to improve your relationship with your children, love them no matter what. If you need relief from your human enemies, astonish them with acts of kindness. The best way to experience maximum strength in our lives is to deliberately choose to walk in love every day. Love is the fruit of the Spirit (see Galatians 5:22). I urge you to die to your selfishness and pray, "Father, I submit to You. Would You create the life of Your Son in me? I exchange my life with His. I allow Your Spirit to control my life and produce the fruit of Your love." He then will begin the process of manifesting His love through you as you rely upon His grace.

You Have Everything You Need

IN HIS CLASSIC work *The Screwtape Letters*, C. S. Lewis observed: "There are two equal and opposite errors into which our race can fall about the devils. One is to disbelieve their existence. The other is to believe, and to feel an unhealthy interest in them."[7] So, what will you do with these weapons of warfare?

One error, Lewis noted, is to disbelieve in the existence of the demonic. Will you minimize the reality of spiritual warfare? Or will you become fascinated with your newfound power, arrogantly thinking of yourself as invincible? Or will you take a third option—become a warrior and use your spiritual weapons under the authority of Christ? We are in a serious battle in this hour. Our human weapons and efforts are not enough to fight our unseen enemies. With these spiritual weapons, we can stop hell's worst and insist on heaven's best.[8] What an honor to have such authority!

As I was fasting and praying for God's insight and direction on the eve of the new millennium, I sensed Him speaking these words: "Everything that you need to be victorious in battle has already been provided to you. Recognize your weapons and use them." I have taken these words to heart and have realized that God's arsenal is essential for the neutralization and destruction of enemy forces. Our skills and weapons will determine whether we are conquerors or casualties. Recognize and use your weapons!

MEN UNDER AUTHORITY

Derek Packard

A mild-mannered pastor once told me about the time he led a ministry team into a spiritually dark place. Witchcraft and violence dominated the area. He recounted how this trip forever shaped his understanding of the authority God gives pastors.

One member of the team was a typical "man's man." A body builder and a decorated veteran, he was highly educated and widely traveled. "He was older than I was and seemed superior to me in every way," my pastor friend explained. "No wonder he didn't respect my leadership. But God had put me in charge."

Because of the dangerous surroundings, the pastor had instructed the group to stay together. But the man left the group one evening without permission and went off alone. Hours later, he returned and ran up to the pastor, exclaiming, "I'm sorry! I'll submit to your authority now!"

"I'll never forget the terrified look in his eyes," the pastor said. "He looked like he'd seen a ghost!"

Who knows? Maybe he came face-to-face with a demon! He never wanted to share the details of what happened, but he recognized his mistake in breaking rank and coming out from under authority. He lost his independent attitude and submitted to his pastor's leadership for the rest of the trip.

An isolated soldier is indeed an easy target for the enemy. Good soldiers follow orders and obey their commander. They operate as a unit. In the same way, our prayer efforts will have the greatest impact if we work as a team under the authority of the Lord and our pastor. Men who don't have that kind of relationship with their pastor (or pastor-appointed prayer leader) are on dangerous ground. They're more susceptible to the attacks of the Enemy and are less effective, because they are not connected to a local church team.

In men's groups at our church, we spend a good percentage of our time praying for those in authority over us, including our pastors, community leaders, and national leaders. This is where the rubber meets the road—where men confess, repent, praise God, make petitions, or just sit still for a few minutes. But we always make time to pray for those in authority over us. By doing this, we obey the apostle Paul's command: "Pray for all people. . . . Plead for God's mercy upon them, and give thanks. Pray this way for kings and all others who are in authority, so that we can live in peace and quietness, in godliness and dignity" (1 Timothy 2:1-2, NLT).

Spiritual Authority

All authority comes from God. Authority grants a person permission to do certain things. Therefore, spiritual authority is permission to act on God's behalf. God speaks to us through the authority of His Word. Pastors use their authority to speak change into our hearts. Police officers maintain peace and order on the authority of civil laws. Obeying authority is fundamental to maintaining order in the universe. Whether it's natural law or the laws of humans, all law ultimately comes from the God who created the whole system of order.

Imagine a busy intersection in your town. The stoplights are working properly, but every driver suddenly begins to ignore the signals and makes his or her own decision on when to go. All sane drivers would soon steer clear of that intersection. Following rules delineated by governing authorities is necessary for any community to function properly. When someone violates the rules, everyone suffers. How much more so in the kingdom of God!

Authority is the permission to tell people to do specific things because "we say so." In practical terms, it is the power to inject your will into a situation and bring change. *Authority* is a tough word to use these days, because American culture frowns on being so direct. Talking forcefully is not politically correct, we are told. For example, at work, the boss is trained to be sensitive to employees' self-esteem when he or she gives a directive. It's quite common to have a team environment at work. Yet there is still the unspoken power of the boss to fire an employee. How can he or she do that? The reason is because the boss intrinsically has the authority to do so.

In the spirit realm, God gives Christians a wide range of authority in spiritual matters. We are like the midlevel supervisors of a corporation. We don't have unlimited authority—only God, the CEO, has that—but He has given us direct power over demonic influences, for example. The problem is, we don't use it. It's like the boss who doesn't seem to know he's in charge. Let's take charge of all the Lord gives to us! But first, we need to get some things in order. As Mario Murillo said, "Before a great awakening, there must come a rude awakening."[1]

Submission to Authority

A true disciple obeys his teacher. God knows your heart by your level of obedience: "If you love me, you will obey what I command" (John 14:15). We men, by nature, don't look for authorities to submit to. Secretly, we would prefer to do things our own way. But the refusal to come under God's authority smacks of pride and rebellion and does not lead to godliness or answered prayer. In fact, it hinders both. Rebellion against any form of authority God has placed in our lives is sin. It may be more subtle than murder, adultery, or drug addiction, but it is a serious affront to God. Scripture even equates rebellion with witchcraft (see 1 Samuel 15:23). That's pretty bad! Weak faith is not rooted in our failure to understand God's principles; it is rooted in our unwillingness to submit completely to Him.

If you feel anemic when you pray, if it seems your prayers never get answered, examine your life for instances of disobedience to authority, including both church and civil leaders. Let's suppose you are divorced and you dislike your ex-wife, so you don't pay your child support. You are disobeying the law of the land and therefore disobeying God. Don't expect much of a prayer life!

Submission and Blessing

According to Scripture, even our father's actions in years past become a legacy of blessings or curses for us. By God's grace, we can start afresh and overcome our negative heritage. Nevertheless, our actions today can affect our children tomorrow. Any man who does not fear God will ultimately leave a legacy of curses for his children (see Exodus 20:5-6). Charles Ryrie explains, "Although there are cumulative effects of sin (cf. Ex. 20:5-6; Matt. 23:35-36), the Lord . . . [in Ezekiel 18:2-4] declares that each individual is accountable for his own sin."[2] We will all answer to God individually, but our obedience to Him and to the authorities He puts over us affects a lot more people than we realize. It affects our family for several generations. When you come to grips with the truth of generational consequences, the impact of learning to obey parental authority, governmental authority, and God's authority takes on greater significance. "Obey the government, for God is the one who put it there" (Romans 13:1, NLT).

The truth is, we need a healthy fear of the Lord as well as a great love for Him. A healthy fear of the Lord motivates us to submit to God during those times when we just don't want to do things His way. As John Bevere is fond of saying, "Submission doesn't even come into play until there is a disagreement."[3] Submission means yielding your rights to the wishes of another. Men in rebellion to authority abdicate their responsibilities and go their own way. I firmly believe you can trace any problem in the world today back to someone who has abdicated his or her responsibility by failing to obey some authority figure. Therefore, the more we obey authority, the fewer problems we will have. Obey God, and you and your family will be blessed!

Submission to the Local Church

Independence will always weaken our prayer effectiveness, but when we submit to our local church, our prayer power is strengthened. In my own experience, I know that when I let a critical attitude distance me from my pastors and church leaders, distance grows between the Lord and me as well. In this hour God is emphasizing how our individual authority flows from linking with our church authority.

God has decentralized His army into units or outposts called local churches, His basic fighting battalions. Just as with the military, a spiritual army can function properly only under leadership.

Unfortunately, too many men are rogue warriors, disconnected from their local church leadership. As Gary Kinnaman noted:

> Tragically, few Christians, especially in North America where we pride ourselves in our individuality, understand our relationship to the whole. Every member of the Body of Christ has a gift and a function; any member detached from his place in the Body is powerless, even lifeless. In fact, there are probably few things more ghastly than a dismembered human body. Perhaps the Lord Jesus feels the same about His Body when the members fight among themselves and everyone does what is right in his own eyes.[4]

I have discovered an amazing truth: my prayers for my family and myself are more effective when I am properly related to the authorities in my church. This is how God designed it to work. The Enemy knows the effectiveness of a united army, so he tempts us in the direction of our natural inclination toward independence. He works to isolate us from the church, and it starts with a critical attitude. Satan wants me to think the church is my enemy. It's an ingenious tactic; when we shoot at each other, we overlook him and he is free to wreak havoc.

Praying for Your Pastor

By now, I hope you are convinced of the importance of submitting to your pastor's leadership. One of the best ways to demonstrate your support of his authority is to pray for him. That's easy if you like him, but what if you don't? How do you pray for a leader you don't respect?

It helps to remember we are praying for the person because of his *position*, not his *performance*. It's a matter of honoring God's chain of command. It's a joy to pray for a leader who thinks the way we do; it's harder to pray for one we find fault with. But God is not interested in our opinion of our pastor's performance; He is interested in our obedience to His Word.

When we detect a problem in those over us, there is a proper way to appeal to them. Jesus explained in Matthew 18:15-17 that we should go to them privately. When we do it God's way, He works through us to bring about a positive change. I like a saying I once heard: If a church wants a better pastor, it can get one by praying for the one it has.

Do pastors really *need* our prayers? According to Peter Wagner, pastors need prayer more than the rest of us. He observes,

> I am convinced that most church members have little or no appreciation of the cost of being a pastor. They know what their pastor looks like and sounds like on the outside, but they have little more idea of what is happening on the inside than they have about what is happening on the inside of their digital watch they look at many times a day.[5]

He believes pastors are specifically targeted by Satan because of their influence and visibility. This is because, "if a pastor falls, more people are hurt and set back in their spiritual lives than if others fall."[6]

In his excellent book on praying for pastors, *Preyed On or Prayed For?* Terry Teykl makes the point with his characteristic wit. "The more people in your church who are praying for your pastor, the fewer will be left to join the firing squad."[7]

I like praying the prayers of the Bible for my leaders. If you want to really bless your pastor, pray Colossians 1:9-12 (NLT) for him:

> We have continued praying for you ever since we first heard about you. We ask God to give you a complete understanding of what he wants to do in your lives, and we ask him to make you wise with spiritual wisdom. Then the way you live will always honor and please the Lord, and you will continually do good, kind things for others. All the while, you will learn to know God better and better.
>
> We also pray that you will be strengthened with his glorious power so that you will have all the patience and endurance you need. May you be filled with joy, always thanking the Father, who has enabled you to share the inheritance that belongs to God's holy people, who live in the light.

This prayer is comprehensive enough to cover most aspects of the pastor's life and ministry, including the following:

- clarity about God's will (verse 9)
- spiritual wisdom (verse 9)
- practical, commonsense wisdom (verse 9)
- a lifestyle that pleases God (verse 10)
- fruitfulness in ministry (verse 10)
- intimacy with the Lord (verse 10)
- endurance in trials (verse 11)
- patience with people (verse 11)
- a joyful, thankful attitude (verse 12)[8]

I think Peter Wagner hit the nail on the head when he said,

Right now, someone you know is in desperate need of your prayers. It's the person out on the front line, leading God's army into the world to proclaim His Good News. The enemy is doing everything he can to stop your leader. But as a Christian, you have been given access to a greater power in this battle: God's intercession.[9]

The Relationship Between Faith and Authority

WHEN WE ARE in proper relationship to God and our spiritual leaders, He is happy to share some of His power with us. But coming under authority does not in itself guarantee a dynamic prayer life; we must add faith to the mix. We must understand that God-ordained authority and faith go hand in hand. The account of the Roman officer who asked Jesus to heal his servant is a perfect example of this:

"I myself am a man *under authority,* with soldiers under me. I tell this one, 'Go,' and he goes; and that one, 'Come,' and he comes. I say to my servant, 'Do this,' and he does it."
    When Jesus heard this, he was astonished and said to those following him, "I tell you the truth, I have not found anyone in Israel with such *great faith.*" (Matthew 8:9-10, emphasis added)

Jesus said the officer had great faith because he understood the power of Jesus' authority. He knew the Lord of heaven and earth only needed to say the word and it would be done. He understood the principle of authority because he lived by it every day.

The case of Jesus' disciples illustrates the power of combining faith and authority. When Jesus sent them out on missionary tours, He equipped them with authority to act on God's behalf. "Calling the Twelve to him, he [Jesus] sent them out two by two and *gave them authority* over evil spirits" (Mark 6:7, emphasis added). Their tours were successful. However, on another occasion they ran into a situation they could not handle by themselves, because it takes more than permission to get the work done; it takes faith as well. While Jesus was going through His Transfiguration, they tried and failed to cast out a demon possessing a boy.

> Afterward the disciples asked Jesus privately, "Why couldn't we cast out that demon?"
>
> "You didn't have enough faith," Jesus told them. "I assure you, even if you had faith as small as a mustard seed you could say to this mountain, 'Move from here to there,' and it would move. Nothing would be impossible." (Matthew 17:19-21, NLT)

Authority gives you permission to move the mountain. Faith is the power to move it. You need both to be an effective warrior in the spiritual realm. On the other hand, having faith but lacking authority can make for a downright embarrassing situation!

> Some Jews who went around driving out evil spirits tried to invoke the name of the Lord Jesus over those who were demon-possessed. They would say, "In the name of Jesus, whom Paul preaches, I command you to come out." Seven sons of Sceva, a Jewish chief priest, were doing this. One day the evil spirit answered them, "Jesus I know, and I know about Paul, but who are you?" Then the man who had the evil spirit jumped on them and overpowered them all. He gave them such a beating that they ran out of the house naked and bleeding. (Acts 19:13-20)

Chuck Kraft writes, "As Jesus' intimacy with the Father was the basis for his authority, so our intimacy with Jesus is the basis for our authority."[10] The sons of Sceva wanted to use the power of Jesus without knowing Him intimately and submitting to His authority. As a result, they suffered the humiliating consequences.

We, too, can open ourselves up to spiritual attack by not being properly related to the Lord and the authorities He has placed in our lives. Remember the man in my opening story—the one who went off by himself in a spiritually dark place? He didn't submit to his pastor's authority and became an easy target for the Enemy.

Who Are You?

Whenever someone receives an order that he is expected to obey, especially if it comes from someone he doesn't know or doesn't respect, he may wonder, *Who are you? What gives you the right to tell me what do?*

If you have children, you've probably witnessed this a time or two. Siblings usually don't enjoy taking orders from one another. But if your child tells his brother or sister, "Do it because Dad said so"—well, that's a horse of a different color!

A similar principle operates in the spiritual realm. The power and authority of Jesus Christ is brought to bear on a situation when we pray "in Jesus' name," because His name represents His authority. The Father gave Jesus all authority. And Jesus chose to give some to His friends. Jesus explained how we can execute the authority He shares with us: "You can go directly to the Father and ask him, and he will grant your request *because you use my name.* You haven't done this before. Ask, *using my name,* and you will receive" (John 16:23-24, NLT, emphasis added).

Just Do It

THE BOTTOM LINE: only a handful of men wield their spiritual authority effectively in their families, churches, and cities. We are ignorant of the authority we have or we are ashamed to use it. Either we are intimidated because our conscience is not clear or we are embarrassed to publicly use the name of Jesus. After all, other people might be offended. Maybe we're just plain afraid to pray with authority.

The Enemy has tricked us into not using a powerful weapon against him. How can we win the war when we soldiers won't use our weapons? The answer is, we can't. And we're not. That's why our churches, communities, and nation are in the shape they are in today. Remember, when we are in proper relationship to the Lord and the authorities He has placed over us, He is happy to share some of His power with us. When we unite and come under the authority of our church, the power He shares with us is increased exponentially: "You will pursue your enemies. . . . Five of you will chase a hundred, and a hundred of you will chase ten thousand, and your enemies will fall by the sword before you" (Leviticus 26:7-8).

When you detect Satan's encroachment in your family, do not be afraid to command him to stop. When he responds, "Why? Who are you?" he is trying to intimidate you. Remind him that your Father gave you permission to tell him, "Back off!"

Part 4

THE MAKING
OF THE
WARRIOR

THE WARRIOR'S HEART

Jim Chosa

I t's 4:00 A.M. and you're sound asleep in your warm bed, dreaming pleasant dreams of your sixth birthday, which is coming in just a few days. Suddenly, you are startled awake as you feel someone's firm grip around your ankle! You struggle to focus your eyes on whoever is yanking you out of bed. You dangle upside down, kicking and squirming, as the dark figure sprints through the blackness, still gripping your ankle. Your mind is racing, trying to make sense of this nightmare, when he finally releases his grip, hurling you into the icy waters of a swiftly moving stream.

What I have just described is a boy's "baptism" into the life of a warrior of the Native American Crow Nation. The father of a male child would place his son under the authority of a skilled and successful warrior. In the days ahead, the boy would repeatedly experience this same baptism. He would be marched to the edge of a nearby stream or river and commanded to strip completely and dive into the cold waters.

The training of the Crow is momentous to me. Even though I was born a full-blood Chippewa, I married into the Crow tribe. Because the Crows are a matriarchal tribe, it's their tradition for the man to become Crow when he marries a Crow woman. He doesn't simply marry an individual; he is adopted into her family. I have spent much time listening to older members of my adoptive Crow family tell stories of the old ways of their tribe before the early 1900s. It was especially fascinating to discover how they developed a warrior's heart in their boys.

Their stories have shown me that something's missing in the church. We need to learn a vital principle from the Crow. To them, warfare was not an option; not to fight meant death and annihilation. Thus warfare became an integral part of the culture of these First Nations people. But Christian men, in general, haven't accepted that warfare is not an option. We haven't faced the fact that Satan has declared war on us.

Committed to War

WHEN WE BECAME believers in Jesus Christ, it's as if we were taken by the ankle and hurled into a war zone where the kingdom of light is clashing violently with the kingdom of darkness. This may come as a surprise to some men. John Wimber described a common misunderstanding that many Christian men experience:

> Often the kingdom [of God] is likened to a Caribbean cruise on a luxury liner. People change into their leisure clothes, grab their suntan lotion, and saunter down to the docks. What a shock it is when they find that entering the kingdom is really more like enlisting in the navy and doing battle with the enemy. . . . The enemy follows no rules of war. Satan considers nothing unfair; he is not a gentleman. The sooner Christians understand this, the more serious they will become about being equipped and properly trained for the kingdom.[1]

I've experienced war firsthand. In 1968 I was drafted into the U.S. Army and sent to Vietnam. I can still hear exploding mortar shells and the crack of the North Vietnamese soldiers' AK-47 rifles. I spent a year of my life in Vietnam. It was a baptism of fire, where the fear of dying almost paralyzed me. As combat infantrymen, we suffered through countless days and nights in the mountainous jungles, which were even more miserable during the monsoon rains. We could not have made it without the commitment and mental toughness of a warrior. Likewise, men, we must have an unwavering commitment to Christ and His cause to be strong spiritual soldiers. In our battles in life, we are to maintain a disciplined warrior's heart. The apostle Paul exhorted timid Timothy to "endure hardship with us like a good soldier of Christ Jesus" (2 Timothy 2:3).

The depth of commitment to war that men of God must make is distinctively modeled by the warrior culture of the Crow Nation. The Crows had a clear recognition of what was at stake if they were not prepared to win the inevitable battles with their enemy. Life against death was the backdrop for every male child born into the tribe. As soon as he was separated from his mother's womb, the male child's gender set his identity and destiny in place. The modern concept of a civilian lifestyle did not exist in the heart and mind of the tribe. Not to submit to the life of a warrior was a display of cowardice of the worst kind.

Beginning with his initial baptism (described above), a boy essentially lost his own life and gained another. He now belonged to the tribe through the stewardship of his mentor. The tribe's destiny was forever linked to the unfolding identity of this child and many like him. Most of the training involved building and anchoring within the heart and mind all the necessary elements of a warrior's heart. We might have expected his training to focus on becoming skilled in the use of the bow and arrow, tracking small game, and playing war games. And these abilities were important parts of the training. However, the training of the heart was the most important element of this process.

Heart Standards for Warriors

FOR THE CROW, the primary goal of the discipleship process was changing the boy's heart by conquering his fear (especially the fear of death) and imparting courage, confidence, and strength. When this emerging warrior reached an age between twelve and fourteen, he would begin to accompany war parties into enemy territory. His first assignment was as a keeper of the campfire and water boy — tasks considered women's work back in the village. The mentor judged his performance more on attitude than ability. Every new

FIGHT ON YOUR KNEES

assignment exposed the young warrior to increasing danger until at last he was participating in actual combat. The mentoring warrior understood the absolute necessity of imparting identity, vision, courage, honor, and humility to the young man. Training was rigorous and repetitive until each element became an instinctive part of the young warrior's heart and mind.

Identity

Growing up in the Chippewa culture, I was introduced to racism early. I discovered that we really didn't know who we were because we had been so influenced by white culture. Even when we played cowboys and Indians, my older brother always got the first choice, and I had to play the Indian.

By the time of my childhood, much of our language had disappeared. The only person I knew who spoke the Chippewa language was my ninety-eight-year-old grandfather. My mother was not allowed to speak her native language or wear her native dress at school. Over the years, I began to wonder, *What is a Chippewa person?*

I was left with feelings of rootlessness. This loss of identity propelled me to research historical documents. I discovered that, after about 1910, the warrior training among First Nations peoples ceased because there was no longer a need. No need for the warrior—that's one of the major reasons why you see so many native men consumed by alcoholism today. Essentially, their identity and destiny have been destroyed.

John Eldredge reminds us,

A man needs a battle to fight; he needs a place for the warrior in him to come alive and be honed, trained, seasoned. . . . A man must have . . . a great mission to his life that involves and yet transcends even home and family. He must have a cause to which he is devoted even unto death, for this is written into the fabric of his being. Listen carefully now: *You do.* That is why God created you—to be his intimate *ally,* to join him in the Great Battle. You have a specific place in the line, a mission God made you for.[2]

Don't flounder because your identity is uncertain. Through Christ, you have access to your heavenly Father, who restores your

126

true identity and makes real your eternal destiny as a firstborn warrior, a son of God.

Vision

For the native warrior, the second heart standard was vision. Success in the battle depended on the discipline and preparation of all the faculties of the warrior's spirit, soul, and physical body. The Crow believed that without a vision a warrior would not be properly prepared for war. The primary means for gaining this vision was the "vision quest." It became a vital element for developing the warrior's spirituality. Vision gave purpose and meaning that guided him through all of life's battles.

The vision quest was essentially a time when the warrior would seek to gain spiritual help and power. He would isolate himself, leaving the village for three or four days. He would lay his weapons down and ask God to show him how much he needed His help. It gave the warrior spiritual power and purpose. We, too, must learn how to get alone with God and ask Him to show us who we are without Him. This brings a spiritual balance to our lives. There is power in God revealing how much we need Him and how He will be there for us.

Honor

Honor was another heart standard of a warrior. The way of a warrior was a life of continuous hardship and sacrifice. It had to be! And these were qualities that were honored, because the very existence of the tribe was carried on the shoulders of its warriors. This way of life, however, had its exhilarating side as well, which centered on "counting coup."

Every time a warrior was able to strike his enemy or take the enemy's weapons or horse, he counted coup. For every coup counted, the warrior was honored with the gift of an eagle feather to wear in his hair. Chief Plenty Coups of the Crow Nation had received much honor in his life and therefore was eligible to wear a very long war bonnet of eagle feathers. But because genuine honor imparts genuine humility, Plenty Coups chose to wear only one feather. Here was a man who could have reveled in his own glory, boasting about his great achievements. Yet he chose the pathway of humility. God's ways follow the path of humility before true honor (see Proverbs 15:33), and true honor then waters the seed of humility. The Crow knew how to give honor to those who deserved it *and* knew how to receive it with humility.

The system of honoring strengthened the warrior culture by enabling young warriors to remain steadfast and true to their callings. When a successful war chief returned to his village, the whole village would turn out and begin to sing his praises for the deeds he had done. All who participated in the campaign shared in the chief's honor. In humility, the chief allowed even the water boy to receive honor.

"Satan . . . is terrified of humility; he hates it," said Francis Frangipane. "He sees a humble person and it sends chills down his back. His hair stands up when Christians kneel down, for humility is the surrender of the soul . . . to the Lord, and the devil is terrified of Jesus Christ."[3]

Courage

An indispensable quality of the warrior's heart is courage. Frangipane reminds us, "God must confront the stronghold of fear within us before we can be effective against the enemy."[4]

When I went to Vietnam, I was called "Chief." I was the "point man," or scout. The others in my unit made the logical assumption, "He's Indian; he'll be our Indian scout." The point man held a unique role in the company. Longevity was not a part of that position, because he was the first one down the trail. If there were an ambush, he was the first casualty. In contrast to the lifelong process of training Crow warriors, we soldiers of the Vietnam War were pushed through boot camp. Consequently, we were not adequately trained for the environment of the jungle, which made us vulnerable. We had to learn quickly, and I thank God that I had several mentors in my platoon.

The following story will help you understand the thick cloud of the fear of death that covered us. We were moving from one mountaintop to a heavily enemy-infested area. I don't think I've ever experienced fear like I did that day, because I could sense the presence of the enemy around me. I was out in front of the company by about five yards. I had my machete in one hand and my M-16 in the other. As we approached our next place to set up for the night, I got word that a bunch of enemy soldiers had been spotted fleeing into the jungle. I had walked right past them. Realizing I had come so close to death, I was flooded with an enormous fear.

The next day, we moved again. This time a different platoon took the lead. Their point man was ambushed and killed. A firefight began that lasted all day. We lost a lot of men but had to go back in again. This time I was the point man. Fear almost immobilized me, but because the platoon leader said, "Go," I went. It was a pivotal challenge, and obedience and submission to my leader made me overcome my fear.

Jesus Christ is your Commander in Chief. When He says, "Go," you can boldly take the next step, knowing He will give you courage to face all kinds of situations.

Security

God opened my eyes to the reality of the spiritual war we enter the moment we say yes to Christ. The memory of Vietnam comes back to me. Every element of that nation was involved in war to one degree or another. God is reminding me how every element of the body of Christ is in war too, whether we know it or not. If we do not become knowledgeable, activated, functioning believers in that warfare, we essentially become POWs.

As I look at the church today, I see many believers sitting in prison camps. They aren't functional, yet they don't realize why the benefits of God are being withheld from them. "Who serves as a soldier at his own expense?" the apostle Paul asked in 1 Corinthians 9:7. No one. The Crow warrior was well supplied by his nation. I didn't go to Vietnam at my own expense; the U.S. military provided everything I needed—transportation, housing, food, clothing, weapons, bullets, and so on. God is saying the same thing to His warriors. He has a reservoir of equipment and provision available, but it will be given only to those who go to war for Him. We can live in the security of knowing that the provision He has made for us is enough to keep us from becoming a casualty in the war.

Wartime Disciplines

FROM THE MODEL of the Crow war culture, we can learn some key biblical principles of discipline and preparation for spiritual warfare. I've chosen three to highlight.

First, when we think of ourselves as being in an army, discipline and preparation become critical issues. Soldiers must live differently than civilians. Like the Crow, Christian men need to eliminate the option of a casual civilian life. Settle it now in your heart: you are a soldier under the authority of Christ. Your marching orders and code of conduct are in the Bible. Let these words soak in: "No one serving as a soldier gets involved in civilian affairs—he wants to please his commanding officer" (2 Timothy 2:4).

Second, our baptism into Christ is our call to a lifestyle of war. As with the Crow boy's "baptism," we essentially lose our life and gain another through our baptism experience. The apostle Paul instructs us, "Don't you know that all of us who were baptized into Christ Jesus were baptized into his death? . . . For we know that our old self was crucified with him so that the body of sin might be done away with, that we should no longer be slaves to sin" (Romans 6:3,6). We must know that by the death of Jesus Christ we can exchange our old life for His life (see Romans 6:11). Like the young warrior, we must be stripped of all our world-stained clothing and jump repeatedly into the river, where our immature attitudes are washed away. Ignorance of being crucified with Christ leaves the door to sin wide open, giving legal access to the deceiving work of the Devil.

Frangipane explained it this way: "We are not trapped in darkness if we have been born of Light. But if we *tolerate* darkness through tolerance of sin, we leave ourselves vulnerable for satanic assault. For wherever there is willful disobedience to the Word of God, there is spiritual darkness and the potential for demonic activity."[5]

To be baptized into Christ is not only to die to our old evil nature but also to "put on Christ" (see Galatians 3:27, NKJV). The Lord Jesus places upon us His warrior's armor of humility, light, and power (see Romans 13:12-14). We lose our old life and now live by Christ's power. As Paul said, "I have been crucified with Christ and I no longer live, but Christ lives in me. The life I live in the body, I live by faith in the Son of God, who loved me and gave himself for me" (Galatians 2:20). In baptism, our old fearful self is left behind in the water. The courageous warrior nature is what emerges when we come up from our baptism.

Third, to prepare for war, we must value mentoring within the church. The First Nations culture understood the importance of the more experienced pouring themselves into the younger men.

Everything in the training process was intentional. Crow fathers took upon themselves the responsibility of finding the best mentors and training for their sons to become successful warriors.

I saw this same desire in my father, who was a lumberjack and trapper. I traveled with him a lot, hunting and trapping. He did his best to instill hunting skills in me, because our family depended on venison and muskrat for food. Even though I grew up in poverty, he also looked out for my future by hammering into my head that I would be the one who would go to college. When he shipped me off to the university, I knew what he was doing—in his own way, he was turning me over to a mentor to prepare me for my future.

Most men in the church today do not think about mentoring the younger men in spiritual warfare and successful Christian living. Most men are preoccupied with their careers or personal issues. Because discipling the next generation doesn't have enough immediate payoff to warrant our focus, it is a neglected aspect of church culture. Somehow we are blinded to the real stakes in the spiritual war we are engaging in. Our negligence in mentoring could cost us a generation.

The Crow father viewed his children as a blessing. It was his responsibility to develop them into strong contributors to the overall society. The Bible teaches this also:

> Children are a gift of the LORD. . . .
> Like arrows in the hand of a warrior,
> So are the children of one's youth. (Psalm 127:3-4, NASB)

The use of "arrows" to describe our children is more than symbolic. I believe this could refer to our descendants becoming greater warriors than we are. They are to be effective and strong soldiers battling our King's enemy:

> Your arrows are sharp. . . .
> Your arrows are in the heart of the King's enemies. (Psalm 45:5, NASB)[6]

I want to see my children live such powerful Christian lives that they are like sharp arrows piercing the forces of darkness that resist our King's will.

Mighty Exploits

TO BECOME A warrior is a matter of the heart. It is a lifelong endeavor, requiring a lifelong commitment.

Let me share a true story out of the history of the Crow Nation that highlights the actions of a warrior, Stump Horn, who on one particular day was fully prepared for battle.[7] In the late 1800s, a Crow hunting party surprised a hunting party of Blackfeet encroaching on their territory in an area called Grapevine Creek. Even though the Crows outnumbered the Blackfeet, the Blackfeet had rifles in addition to bows and arrows. So the Blackfeet chose to stand and fight, building stone breastworks from which to defend themselves. Stump Horn approached the hill singing his war song and zigzagging as an elk does when it runs. He charged the enemy and they shot at him. But they couldn't hit him, and he finally made it to the barricade.

Stump Horn entered the Blackfeet position and began stabbing the occupants, killing two. Demoralized by Stump Horn's apparent invulnerability, the Blackfeet soon broke as other Crow warriors rushed the barricade. Stump Horn seems to have been a typical Crow, thoroughly reputable and well regarded, doing what he had trained his whole life to do.

Just as Stump Horn was a normal warrior in his culture, so we need to see "normal" Christian warriors acting with courage in our culture today. Wouldn't you also like to be a fearless warrior doing mighty exploits? You can be. It is the result of knowing God intimately: "The people that do know their God shall be strong, and do exploits" (Daniel 11:32, KJV).

Join me in prayer, asking that God would impart His warrior heart to us.

Heavenly Father, through Your Son we submit to Your call and Your preparations to enable us to fight the good fight of faith as warriors of Jesus Christ. Transform our hearts and impart to us by Your Word the warrior heart of Christ. Teach our hands to war, and let us be a voice in the wilderness crying out to a lost world, "Prepare ye the way of the Lord." Amen.

THE WARRIOR'S IDENTITY

Harvey Cozzens

" I double-dog dare you to cross that line!" I still remember a few good old-fashioned fistfights from my youth. But nothing compares to the timeless exploits of David the shepherd boy. With one of those "How dare you!" attitudes, David directly confronted the giant Goliath, saying, "You come against me with sword and spear and javelin, but I come against you in the name of the LORD Almighty, the God of the armies of Israel, whom you have defied. This day the LORD will hand you over to me, and I'll strike you down . . . ; for the battle is the LORD's" (1 Samuel 17:45-47). You know the rest of the story. David took a stone, slung it, and struck the giant. Then he took Goliath's sword, killed him, and cut off his head. Does that sound like Sunday school or nice Mister Rogers singing, "It's a beautiful day in the neighborhood"?

Like young David, Christian men are designed, empowered, and called to do mighty exploits as warriors for God.

Let me ask you, have you ever taken a stand to conquer satanic schemes against your soul? Have you stood in the power of His might to defend your wife and children through prayer? Have you fought on your knees for the lost peoples and nations for whom Christ shed

His blood? Given our current social conditions, does a warring spirit rise up in you to fight for the transformation of our nation?

You may say, "Whoa! Wait a minute! I'm still struggling with my sins and who I am. I sure don't see myself as a warrior for God." If so, then it's time you discovered your authentic, God-given identity—the man God designed you to be. Though men come in a wide variety of body and soul packages, within every man is the spirit of a warrior. Most ideas of a warrior are based on folk legends, movie plots, and school yard bullying, but Scripture reveals the true model of a godly, masculine warrior.

Our heavenly Father desires that you come into a full revelation of your true male identity, which will empower you to be a man mighty in prayer. You will experience peace and contentment as you discover who God has designed you to be as a man. Once you grasp the biblical concept of masculine identity, then you can find your destiny through purpose, vision, and mission.

The Plumb Line for True Masculine Identity

IN 1882 MY great-grandfather James B. traveled to Colorado in a covered wagon with his wife, Elizabeth, and their newborn son. This homesteader wore two pistols strapped to his hips—and they weren't just for looks. Back then, men were forced into many masculine responsibilities simply to survive. Not so today. Most men in the twenty-first century cannot define, much less embrace, true masculinity.

Numerous technological advances have given us wonderful benefits, but they have replaced many everyday physical tasks and duties. Something around the house needs repair? We simply call a professional or go to Home Depot for prefab parts. Thus, most men are no longer required to be resourceful and exercise their full physical and creative potential.

Add to this our sociological climate, which distorts authentic masculinity by portraying men as macho dictators or passive wimps, as insensitive spectators, as self-centered recluses, as urban cowboys, and as weekend warriors. Sadly, these caricatures are often true of us males. Our understanding of manhood has also suffered destructive blows through the gender-blurring philosophies that pervade our culture. Tragically, most men don't ask the right questions or take the time to discover and step into their true biblical identity.

The result is that many men have laid down their God-given authority and become complacent spiritual eunuchs and, yes, even prayer eunuchs. I often observe men who have been psychologically and spiritually emasculated. As such, they fail to fulfill the original design and mandate God intended for the sons of Adam. So, what is the godly foundation and plumb line for a genuine masculine identity?

A Chip off the Old Block

Masculinity is a multifaceted dynamic that originated in the heart and nature of God. Becoming a warrior begins with understanding, believing, and embracing the fact that you were made in the image of God.

You know the expression "He's a chip off the old block." Both my adult sons are clearly my sons, chips off this old block. They look, sound, and think much like I do. People frequently say to each of them, "You must be Harvey's son." What's true in the physical world is strikingly true in the spiritual realm as well: we actually resemble our heavenly Father. That is because, in the beginning, God said, "Let Us make man in Our image, according to Our likeness; and let them rule. . . . God saw all that He had made, and behold, it was very good" (Genesis 1:26,31, NASB).

So, what does image and identity have to do with being a godly warrior? Everything! By the grace of God, once you've successfully assimilated His blueprint for authentic biblical masculinity, you can become the warrior He has *created* and *expects* you to be.

God's Image, My Image

Let's look closer at the image of God and, in so doing, lay a foundation for our own image. One way we can come to intimately know God's nature and character is by understanding His names and titles. Your identity as a warrior designed in His image becomes more evident as you look at the richness of God's various warrior titles. Take Exodus 15:3, for example. Here God is described as a man of war. Various Bible translations expand this concept and call Him a warlike one, mighty in battle, the Eternal who knows well how to fight, the warrior God. To make sure we get it, the Bible uses at least four more warrior titles for God:

- *Jehovah-Sabaoth*—the Lord of hosts[1] (1 Samuel 17:45). He is the Supreme Commander in Chief of the armies of heaven and earth.
- *Jehovah-Nissi*—the Lord our banner[2] (Exodus 17:15). He is the one who goes victoriously before us into battle.
- *Jehovah-Shalom*—the Lord our peace[3] (Judges 6:24). Jesus Christ is the Prince of Peace, and the warrior's primary role is to maintain the peace.
- *El Gibbor*—mighty warrior[4] (Deuteronomy 10:17). He is the strongest force in the universe.

These titles allow us to discover who we are because we are created in God's image. Then, by faith, we can activate protection from Satan's intimidating attacks against our genuine identity. Because God is clearly a warrior, I, too, as one made in His image, have the genes of a warrior.

Let me illustrate. When I am feeling fearful, passive, or unmotivated to plunge into the battles of life, I ponder God's warrior titles and conclude that I am a soldier who serves in an army under the Lord, my Supreme Commander in Chief. He is the leader who goes into battle before me; therefore, He wants me to have an expectation of victory. Knowing who I am biblically strengthens me when cultural seductions sing to me like sirens, luring me away from my God-given identity.

Behavior as a Function of Perception

I GREW UP on a farm, and many times my dad took me out behind the big red barn to adjust my perception. Sure enough, my behavior changed! Behavior is a function of perception, or in other words, you do what you believe. The Bible also describes this truth: "As he thinks in his heart, so is he" (Proverbs 23:7, NKJV). It is imperative to understand God's intent for manhood before you will be able to live as a godly warrior. I know that, like me, you have a deep yearning for an exhilarating life full of challenge, power, romance, freedom, and eternal impact. This yearning signals a desire to return to God's original design for our lives.

Before you read any further, let's go behind the big red barn. I want to remind you that most men fall woefully short of God's design for their lives because of disobedience, rebellion, and pride. Therefore, I challenge you to repent from any sinful habits and commit to a personal quest to find your God-given identity. Reclaim and reestablish your heart as a servant-warrior of God. David the warrior-king had his day in the sun. Now it's our time! Our battle! One of my deepest passions is that it would be said of you and me, as it was of King David, that we are men after God's heart. May we obey His commands, fulfill His will and purposes, and serve our generation (see Acts 13:22,36).

Four Facets of Godly Manhood

The discovery I'm about to share with you has brought clarity, peace, and confidence to me as a man, as a husband, and as a father. Like God, we are much more than warriors—more than just people who can grow hair on our faces, lift heavy objects, and act tough when threatened.

So, what else does masculinity encompass? We need go no further than the Gospels to find the archetype of authentic masculinity. Christ's nature, revealed in the four Gospels, is a complete picture of God's design for men. God wants us to manifest the same four facets that are woven into the fabric of His Son's manhood: the king, the warrior, the lover, and the prophet.

King: wise nobleman worthy of honor and respect. In the gospel of Matthew we find our authority to rule revealed in Christ as the King (see Matthew 2:2). He is characterized as a steward and head of the kingdom—one who is a wise and benevolent leader. The king in Christ, and the king in you, is to be honored and respected. God designed humans in His image to rule the earth as viceroys, or His representatives (Genesis 1:28). The king in you is one who blesses, encourages, and cares deeply for others. As a king, you have two primary responsibilities: to love the Lord your God and to love your neighbor as yourself.

Reared in an agricultural community, I watched in awe as my grandfathers, father, and uncles lived out bigger-than-life examples of what it means to *be* and *do* as kings over their domains. There was never any doubt who was in charge. They were strong, organized, and generous. Though often pushed to the breaking point, they were unwavering.

We, too, have "kingdoms" (realms of responsibility, such as homes and businesses) worth fighting for. The driving motivation of a king in our genetic makeup enables us to release wisdom and protection over those kingdoms. God wants this regal self-assessment to replace our insecurities with a deep sense of dignity and worth.

How should this kingly aspect shape our prayers? You, as a godly king, can pray *with boldness and authority* in humility and dependence upon your heavenly Father.

Warrior: fearless servant aggressively fighting for peace and justice. The gospel of Mark reveals the warrior energy of Christ. This gospel of action emphasizes what Jesus did more than what He said (see Mark 2:22,27). Christ walked on water, fed thousands, condemned the Pharisees, and taught as one having great authority. He demonstrated His power over demons, disease, storms, and even death. Christ clearly had warrior components in His mission: "The Son of God appeared for this purpose, to destroy the works of the devil" (1 John 3:8, NASB). You, too, are to be a servant devoted to causes greater than your own personal survival.

The warrior in Christ and in us is characterized first as a peacekeeper who defends the oppressed and those under attack. Then he moves toward reforming society—based on truth and justice. He exhibits righteous aggressiveness, courage, discernment, and decisive action. Adapting well to changing situations and environments, he is a strategist and tactician. These may seem like lofty goals, but they come into play regularly in everyday life.

My son Chris, as a seventh grader, pushed two required reading books across the dinner table, saying, "Dad, I can't read these." After reviewing the books, I understood my son's concerns. Not only were they filled with profanity, but also they portrayed witches and warlocks as respectable role models. The righteous warrior rose up in me. I presented my concerns to the school administration, and they saw my point and disciplined the teacher. I still remember that stressful experience and the strong emotions that stirred in me as I stepped into my warrior role.

How does the warrior aspect affect your prayers? You, as a godly warrior, can pray *aggressively* in humility and dependence upon your heavenly Father.

Lover: compassionate man in touch with humanity's needs. The third fascinating dynamic of manhood is found in the gospel of Luke. In deep compassion the Son of Man offers salvation to the whole world. Luke focused on Jesus relating to individuals (see Luke 19:1-10; 23:39-43). He gave a prominent place to women. We get a glimpse into Christ's birth and childhood and the thoughts of his mother, Mary. The stories of the penitent thief, the prodigal son, and the good Samaritan passionately come alive. Now, stick with me, because the lover in you is a vital component of a great warrior.

Love brings unique meaning to our lives. Love sees with high sensitivity. It feels with compassion and empathy. Because of love, Jesus, the mighty Warrior-King, wept over Jerusalem and humanity. Love involves multifaceted joy and pain. It bears all things and endures all things. Love never fails (see 1 Corinthians 13:7-8). It is love that humanizes your role as king and warrior. Without love, the king would not have a legitimate reason to rule, the warrior would not have the passionate motivation to defend the peace for his loved ones.

Consider testosterone. This hormone causes a man to have strength and exhibit fierce, competitive warrior traits. Yet it also drives a man's passions toward gentle, sensitive romance. Go figure. It's God—the omniscient, omnipotent Creator of the universe—who designed it that way!

How does the lover in you shape your prayers? You, as a godly lover, can pray *compassionately* in humility and dependence upon your heavenly Father.

Prophet: spiritually sensitive man obeying God's Word. Last, let's look at the gospel of John. Here we find the fourth powerful pillar of masculinity—the prophet, the spiritual dynamic of man who intimately connects with God as Father. By the word "prophet," I do not mean the office of a prophet, nor do I mean the gift of prophecy. I'm referring to a man who is mighty in word and deed like Jesus.

This is an aspect of sonship in which we hear God's Word, speak God's Word, and obey God's Word (see John 8:28-29). The apostle Paul declares our sonship in these words: "Those who are led by the Spirit of God are sons of God" (Romans 8:14).

During Creation, the Lord put in people's spirit the ability to connect with His Spirit. Wow! The prophetic aspect allows us to be in touch with God by hearing and proclaiming His Word. Through that connection, we receive spoken words from Him. The Greek language of the New Testament uses the word *rhema* for God's word spoken to our spirits. His gentle leadings come to us in words that give guidance and peace. This blessed communication process gives you counsel with the omniscient Lover of your soul. His sovereign design enables you to walk supernaturally in every area of your life as a king, warrior, lover, and prophet.

The gospel of John is rich with the theology and reality of Christ's deity as the Son of God. It also reveals an intimate relationship of Christ the Son walking with His Father. As God's adopted sons, we too can have a close relationship with Him. Key phrases throughout John are critical to your understanding your identity and walk with God:

- "To those who believed in his name, he gave the right to become children of God." (1:12)
- "I have come . . . to do the will of him who sent me." (6:38)
- "He who belongs to God hears what God says." (8:47)
- "If you remain in me and my words remain in you, ask whatever you wish, and it will be given you." (15:7)

I have discovered during the last three decades the amazing adventure of hearing God's voice and walking with Him. This supernatural life—whether negotiating a real estate contract, parenting, or teaching—has been possible only as I have stayed sensitive to God's Spirit. In all areas of my life, I have learned the necessity of hearing God's *rhema* before making a decision.

How does the prophet in you affect your prayers? You, as a godly prophet, can pray *with the Holy Spirit's guidance* in humility and dependence upon your heavenly Father.

The Process God Uses to Mature Men

ALL OF US have a kingly, warrior, lover, and prophetic genetic code. They form the DNA upon which God begins great testing and developing. As God matures us, He brings balance to these four dimensions of our masculinity. For example, if we are functioning too much in the kingly area, we will tend to be harsh, domineering, and insensitive. Or if we are operating too much in our lover aspect, we will tend to be passive and not wrestle with difficult issues. The mature, godly man has all four aspects flowing together. He is a strong leader who lovingly serves and fights for the rights of those around him under the guidance of God's Spirit.

The Hebrew culture and language of the Old Testament can help us understand the process God uses to mature men. Six Hebrew words define our masculine identity in terms of various phases of life. Robert Hicks, in his insightful book *The Masculine Journey*, delineated the stages of manhood through these six Hebrew words. You will find his explanations, summarized below, a liberating and enriching revelation of the transitions you encounter on your masculine pilgrimage.

Adam: *the creational male.* The first word to define all humankind in general is *adam.* Hicks explains, "We are not derived from ourselves, nor do we live exclusively for ourselves, but we . . . reflect our Creator."[5] Thus, we have eternal significance because of our link with the eternal Creator. By sovereign design, we are relational beings and must not live in isolation. Creativity and a sense of meaning and mission are inherent qualities in the sons of Adam.

Zakar: *the phallic male.* The second word, Hicks says, defines maleness "in its most base, fundamental anatomical aspect. To describe men as phallic beings recognizes . . . a critical aspect of maleness, . . . which either gets denied, denigrated, or perverted in our culture. . . . To be male is to be a phallic kind of guy, and as men we should never apologize for it."[6] Nevertheless, in this stage we need to understand God's grace for us to harness our passions and become self-controlled sexual beings.

Gibbor: *the warrior. Gibbor* refers to a man's genetic code of strength for battle. "This competitive warring is also a part of being a man. . . . The important question is . . . whether . . . they are fighting for the right things. Strength, combat, and competition are masculine traits, and unless they are . . . valued . . . in our society we are in serious trouble."[7] If a society doesn't have warriors for defense and protection, history shows that it will not be able to survive. Godly men must learn that our drive for combat finds its highest expression on our knees in intercessory prayer as we cover our families and battle the forces of darkness.

Enosh: *the wounded male.* This is probably the most insightful of all Hicks's designations for masculinity. He notes that *enosh* "describes man in his weakness . . . and in his woundedness. . . . He has been wounded by abusive and absent fathers; by domineering mothers and teachers . . . in business . . . by failure . . . by success."[8] Tragically, many men never progress beyond this point because their wounds become the dominating focus of their life. God uses this season of disillusionment and heartache to draw us to Him for restoration and healing. Men who successfully embrace God's healing and walk through this difficult and necessary step find the next two phases rewarding.

Ish: *the mature man. Ish,* observes Hicks, "reflects man as the ruler of his own soul . . . one who is his own man, who knows who he really is and what he is all about, apart from anyone else."[9] This word describes the redeemed warrior who has suffered and been scarred but has survived and now is ready to develop into greater maturity. The *ish* can more clearly hear God's voice as he approaches life with seasoned wisdom. This stage can be the most fulfilling and fruitful for a man, for he now grasps the significance of life. He is alive to the Spirit and dead to his own desires.

Zaken: *the sage.* The last stage is reflected in a word that means, literally, "gray-headed." Hicks further explains that *zaken* includes "the idea of the wise mentor or *sage* . . . making his finest and most important contribution to the community. . . . Our sages today have either been scorned into hiding or they don't exist."[10] We do, indeed, tend to ignore and dismiss our elders. The biblical model, however, encourages us to respect and tap into their wisdom (see Proverbs 16:31; 20:29). A healed and restored older, godly man is poised to release his counsel and wisdom. He is ready to live fully as a king, warrior, lover, and prophet.

These six words embody the process common to all men who are becoming useful servants of God. As you see where you are in this journey, be encouraged! The Lord will not leave you stuck in one phase so long as you choose to cooperate with His grace. He will take all the time needed to bring you into a place of fulfillment and impact.

Mighty Together

EARLY ONE MORNING I heard in my spirit, "We are mighty together." God and I mighty together? I was awed and wonderfully overwhelmed. Yet instantly I knew I was mighty, not in myself, but together with God—in Christ.

O man of God, you *are* mighty! You are created in God's image. You have been divinely designed and supernaturally empowered. Take your post and stand as a warrior of God. March toward your authentic masculine calling. The expressions of authentic masculinity are many and diverse. President George W. Bush, Billy Graham, Kurt Warner, and you are all warriors. As I noted earlier, men come in a variety of body-and-soul packages. But in the spirit, let there be no doubt, every born-again man is a warrior. Yet the choice to stand as a warrior is every man's alone.

Now, with an understanding of your image and identity come purpose and responsibility. You have a kingdom to rule, battles to win, a beauty to love, and an eternal cause—one that goes beyond your family and culture—to champion. God created you to be His ally to stand and reign with Him now and throughout the ages. Just listen to this thunderous climax from the final pages of the Bible: "I saw heaven opened, and behold, a white horse, and He who sat on it is called Faithful and True, and in righteousness He judges and wages war. . . . And the armies which are in heaven, clothed in fine linen, white and clean, were following Him on white horses" (Revelation 19:11,14, NASB). These verses place you and me right in the fury and thick of the battle. We are Christ's fellow warriors! This prophecy is going to be fulfilled, and we get to participate!

Can you ride a white horse? Whose side do you want to ride on? I've made my choice—I want a piece of the action! Now the choice is yours. Cowboy *up!* Let's ride!

CALL TO WAR

Bill McCartney

Why do we need a call to war? In 1904 S. D. Gordon knew why:

> The greatest agency put into man's hands is prayer. And to define prayer one must use the language of war. Peace language is not equal to the situation. The earth is in a state of war and is being hotly besieged. Thus one must use war talk to grasp the facts with which prayer is concerned. Prayer from God's side is communication between Himself and His allies in enemy country.[1]

When President George W. Bush called the nation to war, I knew the Lord was also trying to get the church's attention. I took it as a signal that the church was supposed to go to war in a greater way than we've ever experienced. We've got to wake up the men of God. They need to be stirred up!

In a time of war, when we have soldiers defending our physical beings overseas, God would say to the men back home, "I need you to go to war. I need you, through prayer, to raise up a godly standard in a time of great difficulty." No country can depend solely on the might of its military to protect it, for as a psalmist says,

I do not trust in my bow,
    my sword does not bring me victory;
    but you give us victory over our enemies,
    you put our adversaries to shame. (Psalm 44:6-7)

Guys, do you know what time it is? It's late, very late. Our prayer lives can't be business as usual anymore. If we only look after ourselves, we may lose a generation for the cause of Christ. We need to be men who stand and fight, but in this war we fight in prayer. Dick Eastman reminded us of prayer's power:

> History proves, beyond question, that prayer can change the world. A prayer warrior, on his knees, involves himself in a mission capable of altering the very destiny of men and nations. When the great Reformation swept Europe in the 16th and 17th centuries it was sparked by much prayer. The Huguenots had been instrumental in bringing revival to France but the enemies of the cross, in a dreadful purge called St. Bartholomew's Massacre, destroyed most of the Christians. The nation of France never recovered and finally drifted into a bloody revolution.
>
> A similar thing might have happened in Scotland, had it not been for John Knox. We recall his prayer, "Give me Scotland or I die." Prayer again helped alter history.
>
> A study of past revival in England reveals the same. Great Britain was rapidly slipping into the condition of her French neighbor. But John and Charles Wesley, along with George Whitefield, began those historic prayer meetings, and a mighty revival resulted for England. Once more prayer altered the course of history.[2]

When I travel across the country calling men to war, I sense that this call is going over the heads of most. Some men can't wait for me to stop talking about it so they can get back to what they were doing. That's because a call to war changes everything. It causes you to step back and reexamine everything you're doing. During a war, you have to decide what is really important.

In a time of war, you ration supplies, you're alert, you're ready to move at a moment's notice. But in this war most Christian men are AWOL. Sure, they are showing up for church, but they are not on active duty. We're living like we're at peace. We've put our spiritual pursuits on cruise control. Pastor Ted Haggard sized up the situation like this: "A wartime army is a little sharper than a peacetime army. A peacetime army can get a little peaceful, slouch around a little bit, wondering if they'll ever get in a real battle. We are in a real battle for our nation and for freedom in our world!"[3]

The church has been *in* a war all along, but we haven't been *at* war. We've been living like we're in peacetime. After the tragic events of September 11, 2001, we witnessed a dramatic increase in people attending prayer meetings. But a month or so later, churches slipped back to normal. While we are the church at peace, the Devil is on the move. If we want to see our nation change, we now have a window of opportunity. With all the instability in the world, what are we to do? If you are a Christian, this call to war is inside you. It is resonating with your spirit. And I want you to know that you, as one man, are not powerless. You can make a big difference.

What Does a Warrior Look Like?

KING DAVID WAS only one man. But God used him to serve His purpose in his generation (Acts 13:36). God described David as "a man after my own heart; he will do everything I want him to do" (Acts 13:22). David wanted to be intimate with God. He was far from perfect; he struggled just like you and me. In fact, he committed some horrible sins. But he came back to God (2 Samuel 11–12). What distinguished David from other men was his passionate heart after the Lord. Yet he didn't stop there. God said David would do "everything I want him to do." He had more than just fire and passion; he was obedient and humble.

Someone has said, "An adventure is where you go somewhere and come back, but a quest is where you go somewhere and you may never come back." Guys, I'm suggesting that we go on a quest for God's heart and never come back. "One thing I ask," David wrote in Psalm 27:4—only *one* thing: "All the days of my life, I want intimacy with God" (paraphrased). That's what David lived for. He wanted to *know* God and *talk* with Him. That's what marked David as a man after God's own heart. God is calling for a whole heart. He promised that wholehearted seekers will find Him. "You will seek me and find me when you seek me with all your heart" (Jeremiah 29:13). There's not a man reading this who can't fit the description of David and do the following: (1) be a man after God's heart, and (2) do all His will. It begins as a decision of your will, and then God's grace will empower you to follow through. It simply means being a guy who's after His heart and will do what He tells him to do.

You may be thinking, *What was David really doing when he spent so much time praying?* He was getting close to the Lord. He said, "That's where I get my confidence. I spend time with God. I cry out to God. God speaks to me. I know Him. I walk with Him and talk with Him." That marks a man of God. Today God is looking for men to stand up and recognize the day we live in and rise to the occasion—men who shake off lethargy and passivity and go after Him!

A lot of guys have good intentions but don't follow through. David was obedient to the end. That's why God singled him out. Remember, David wasn't more than a man. He was a great sinner like you and me, but God singled him out because he finished what he started. Will you go the distance with God? Will you obediently follow through on the things the Lord tells you to do?

Whatever the Cost

A FIRE BURNS in the guy who spends time with God. "Draw near," the Lord says. We are to "feel [our] way toward him and find him" (Acts 17:27, NLT). It's a picture of a mountain climber. His foot is locked in. He's reaching with his hand to get to a higher level. Finally his hand is locked in. He finds a foothold, braces himself, then starts to inch up with his other hand. That's it! That's what God wants. "Come after Me. Keep coming and closing the gap between us, because I'll close it faster than you, if you'll just keep moving toward Me."

Nobody said it's going to be smooth. It's hard. It's a daily discipline. It requires more than changing our perspective; we have to change our schedules, too. The word *mediocre* means "halfway." We need churches filled with guys who want *all* of God—men who don't stop halfway up the mountain, men who lose some sleep to spend time with the Lord.

Men need a scoreboard. When a guy knows what the end looks

like, he'll pay a great price to get there. Where there's no vision, men cast off restraint (see Proverbs 29:18). When a man can't see what the end looks like, he doesn't try as hard. To help us see the end, we need to pray, "Teach us to number our days" (Psalm 90:12).

Here is the end of history: Jesus is coming back in glory to gather everybody who has ever believed in Him (see Matthew 24:30-31). He is going to say: "Come, you who are blessed by my Father; take your inheritance, the kingdom prepared for you since the creation of the world" (Matthew 25:34). That means you get it all—everything the Father has. That's what the end looks like! It's worth everything. We get to be with Him forever. It's worth our going back to Him in prayer day after day and being red-hot embers, obedient to go after God like the mountain climber.

During the 2001 Stanley Cup playoffs, in his last game for the Colorado Avalanche, Ray Bourke said, "I want the cup. I'll do whatever it takes." And he did. Get your eyes on the prize of knowing God passionately. Pay whatever the price is to pull it off. In the book of Acts, Barnabas was visiting some new Christians and he left them this piece of advice: "Stay close to the Lord, whatever the cost" (11:23, TLB).

God Is Looking for a Few Good Men

GOD WANTS MEN after His heart, men who are going for Him, men who are serious. He is a rewarder of those who diligently seek Him (see Hebrews 11:6). What the church needs is *fire*. If you get a few guys torched, the rest will get torched. When I coached, I realized that in any group roughly ten players were capable of leading that team. Another ten were going to resist and deny every positive idea that was presented. The eighty guys in the middle would go either way. If those ten leaders truly had fresh fire and deep humility, they could pull the eighty where they didn't necessarily know how to go or want to go. Show me a guy who is on fire for the Lord and who balances that with deep humility, and I will show you a guy who can influence the men in his church and city. A fire is burning in the guy who spends time with God, who draws near to Him. Remember, it doesn't take many men, because the guy who is torched by God will torch others.

Historically, women have carried the prayer ministry in churches. It's time men helped to shoulder the burden of prayer.

God is waiting for His *men* to show up:

- "I want *men* everywhere to lift up holy hands in prayer" (1 Timothy 2:8, emphasis added).
- "*Men* always ought to pray and not lose heart" (Luke 18:1, NKJV, emphasis added).
- "I am a *man* of prayer" (Psalm 109:4, emphasis added).
- "The prayer of a righteous *man* is powerful and effective" (James 5:16, emphasis added).

So, where are you? Are you still on spiritual milk? Most Christian men are. I want to ask you a question. Where would your church be if every man were as devoted as you are to seeking the Lord? If every man's personal time with the Lord were identical to your prayer time, would your church be dramatically different?

As I write, I feel like we are in the middle of a game. We are together in the locker room at halftime and play is suspended for a short while. We have to reassess where we're going. Here's where we're headed: God is calling *men* to pray! *Men* need to pray for their families, churches, pastors, cities, nation, and world. God is looking for a few good men—men who are armed and ready for battle, like the mighty men with King David (1 Chronicles 12:23-38, NKJV). They were

- equipped for war (verse 23)
- armed for war (verse 24)
- men of valor, fit for war (verse 25)
- valiant warriors (verse 28)
- loyal (verse 38)
- mighty men (verse 30)
- understanding of the times, knowing what to do (verse 32)
- stouthearted men who could keep ranks (verses 33, 35)
- fighting men (verse 38)
- undivided, that is, of one mind (verse 38)

These were men of unwavering commitment. God wants mighty men in His army like the mighty men in David's army. The church needs that kind of men! The church has always gone to battle on the knees of its prayer warriors, especially on the knees of its praying men.

With the current threats against our nation and the lethargic state of the church, we are in a serious battle. And men have been chosen to be on the front lines of that battle. Praying men are the mightiest force in the universe, and our most powerful weapon to win great victories is prayer.

We need an unflinching attitude like Napoleon had. He was just a little guy, but he was a leader. Listen to what Napoleon said: "The enemy is in front of us. They're behind us. They're on our right flank and they're on our left flank. There's no way we can miss them now!" That's where we are, guys. Everywhere we turn, there's an opportunity. God is ready to do a mighty work. He's waiting for us to stand up and be men. We are not to build a bypass when Satan throws up a mountain of resistance against us; we are to challenge him and hurl his mountain into the sea (see Matthew 17:20). We are not to hold the fort until Jesus comes; we are to storm the gates of hell, and God has promised that they will not prevail against us (see Matthew 16:18).

Ask God to light a holy fire in your soul by the power of the Holy Spirit, to transform your praying from weakness to prevailing power. The disciples once asked, "[Jesus,] teach us to pray" (Luke 11:1). He began, "Our Father." He led them to the Father. Later, He went to the cross and tore open the veil: "At that moment [His death] the curtain of the temple was torn in two from top to bottom" (Matthew 27:51). It's as if Jesus were telling the disciples, "Now go and have intimacy with My Father. I've been telling you about Him; now go and be with Him, spend time with Him."

Let's not skip over this too quickly. To understand the implications of what really happened, we must look at the background of the temple. Once a year, the high priest entered into the most sacred area of the temple, called the Holy of Holies. This was where God's presence dwelt. The high priest was the only person allowed entrance. A curtain separated the Holy of Holies from a less sacred place, the Holy Place. When Jesus died, the curtain was literally torn. No more separation! That gave all of us free access to go into the most intimate place to be with God the Father. What an extreme privilege!

He knows every hair on your head (see Matthew 10:30). He will wipe every tear from your eyes (see Revelation 21:4). He didn't say the angels will do it; He will do it personally. That's a God who wants intimacy. That's a God who will give you a fire in your heart. If you spend time with Him, nothing will be the same. Everything's going to change.

We have the opportunity every day to be purged and cleansed. There isn't any man who can't find God if he wants Him. I don't care what your schedule is. I haven't set an alarm clock in three years; I can't wait to get up to meet Him.

You Can Do It!

WHEN I WAS a coach, we had a chant: "Good, better, best. Never let it rest till your good is your better and your better is your best." That says it. God wants the same for all of us. No one has arrived. No one should be satisfied. No one knows God so intimately that he's had enough of Him. I want fresh fire and deep humility, and I want to finish everything I've started for God.

The church is *in* a war but not *at* war. The church is being called to war, but many men are missing it. The church is present but not on active duty. When the call comes to fight the good fight of faith, where are the men? Where are you in this battle? God is calling the church to wake up!

When you close this book, I implore you, start praying with your wife every day. Every day, pray over your kids. Find a group of guys and start praying. But most important of all, decide you're going to let God shape you—through personal, intimate, consistent prayer—into a man totally after His heart.

This is doable. It's not impossible. Start by getting on your knees. Men, if we don't wake up, we're going to lose this generation—and that's your kids I'm talking about. In a time of great crisis, Nehemiah issued this call to war: "Don't be afraid. . . . Remember the Lord, who is great and awesome, and fight for your brothers, your sons and your daughters, your wives and your homes" (Nehemiah 4:14).

I want to ask you again, why a call to war? Paul Billheimer knew why: "The church holds the balance of power in world affairs. . . . Even now, by means of . . . prayer power and the extent to which [we use] it, the praying church is actually deciding the course of human events."[4] Put prayer to work and you will see God work in you, your family, your community, your church, and the nation.

PASTORS' STRATEGIES FOR MOBILIZING MEN TO PRAY

Phil Miglioratti

"Without a vision, the warriors perish" (Proverbs 29:18, my paraphrase). In every war, soldiers need generals who sound the battle call clearly and loudly. Spiritual warfare is no different. Men must be summoned to the fight by a visionary leader, and that leader should be their pastor.

If men are going to effectively fight on their knees, they will need pastors who take spiritual warfare and strategic prayer personally and seriously. Victory requires a new breed of shepherd—one who leads the way into the arena of prayer. And every victory is the result of a comprehensive strategy.

Strategy 1—The Man

PASTORING HAS CHANGED dramatically in the last fifty years. One of the clearest indications is how the sign on the pastor's door has

FIGHT ON YOUR KNEES

changed from Study to Office. The pastor is now more a manager or corporate executive officer than a student or a disciple.

A call to war is a call to change. Pastors must reclaim their role as one who leads the troops into battle (see Joshua 5:13–6:27). They cannot do this solely from the boardroom; they must lead both *from* and *into* the prayer room. Our spiritual leaders must rediscover and reclaim the apostles' passion for prayer and the Word (see Acts 6:4).

Crucial Questions

- Pastor, what do you need to change in your schedule in order to be devoted to prayer (see Colossians 4:2)?
- Will you commit to strengthening your personal prayer life by reading a book on prayer? attending a prayer training conference? participating in a pastors' prayer group?[1] Who can you trust to hold you accountable when you share this commitment with them?

Creative Activities

- Take your calendar (or Palm Pilot) and add a one-hour appointment, one day a week, for the next five weeks.
- Divide the appointment between reading on prayer, journaling on prayer (your personal observations), writing on prayer (articles for the church bulletin or newsletter), and of course praying.

Strategy 2 — The Message

WARRIORS NEED A battle plan, and they must receive clear instructions from the teaching ministry of their pastor (see 1 Corinthians 14:8). Prayer must become the topic of sermons and messages, the focus of class and group study, the example and illustration in teaching and preaching. For too long, prayer has been the one thing we have not taught new believers (nor veterans, for that matter). We assume they must know how to pray because they "prayed to receive Christ." Prayer has been unused and misused because the leaders have not trained soldiers in this weapon of war (see 2 Corinthians 10:4; Ephesians 6:18).

154

Crucial Questions
- Pastor, when can you next preach on prayer? Will it be a single sermon? a series?
- How can you best survey your congregation about prayer? Ask them to tell you their most significant questions, problems, and hopes about prayer in regard to their personal life and the life of the church.

Creative Activities
- Go surfing online to find prayer resources: books, teaching videos, networks. A good place to start is www.nalcpl.net.
- Schedule a planning session with those who make curriculum choices for your church ministries. Devote 50 percent of the meeting to prayer and 50 percent to discerning how the Lord wants the church to be taught about prayer. Apply what you discover to sermons, Sunday school classes, small groups, Bible studies, and the various ministries of the church (youth, children, singles, couples, and seniors).

Strategy 3 — The Motivation

PRAYER IS ESSENTIAL because it is essential, not because it is the latest topic or trend and not because the pastor read a book or attended a conference and now feels guilty. For men to fight on their knees, they will require more than a battle *call*; they must have a battle *cry*. They must grasp the reason, pulsate with the passion, and embrace the vision. A battle cry is loud, not simply to catch everyone's attention, but to express deep desire and desperation. A pastor who wants to lead his men into battle must have a cry, a burden; he cannot simply make an announcement.

Our motivation is the call and the cry of our Lord and Leader in John 17:3-4: "Now this is eternal life: that they may know you, the only true God, and Jesus Christ, whom you have sent. I have brought you glory on earth by completing the work you gave me to do."

Our motivation? A desire for the church to complete the work God has given us to do—so that those who do not know the only true God would receive eternal life through faith in Christ, and so that God would receive glory on earth. The battle and the victory are all for God. We fight with and for the Creator of the universe. Our cry: "Jesus rules! To hell with evil! God loves the world!"

Crucial Questions

- Pastor, how can you make teaching and preaching about prayer a motivating experience for your congregation?
- Does your congregation know the ultimate purpose of prayer (not to change circumstances but to bring glory to God)? If not, how would making that paradigm shift change their praying?

Creative Activities

- During the next three weeks, attend every prayer meeting you can. Identify what makes the meeting motivational or what makes it boring and irrelevant. Review your observations for the purpose of revising prayer in your congregation and using it effectively at different points. During weeknight prayer meetings? Committee and board meetings? Church services? Sunday and weekday classes?
- Take a group of men on a prayer journey through Scripture. Skim the book of Acts, stopping at each "prayer meeting" to determine what motivated the early Christians to come to the place of prayer and what kept them there. Ask your men what would help them to begin praying with the same vibrancy and conviction seen in the book of Acts.
- Next time you have an appointment with the Lord, ask the Holy Spirit to give you ideas for motivating men to pray.

Strategy 4 — The Model

MEN WILL NOT follow a man who simply teaches them about prayer, but they will die with a man they see and hear in prayer. Christian men are looking for a leader who is unafraid to plunge into the deeper waters of communication and cooperation with God.

The most eloquent sermon is powerless if the preacher cannot supply the evidence of personal experience, both success and failure. The most gifted teacher cannot persuade men to change their lifestyle if he has not done the same in the crucible of prayer.

Crucial Questions
- Pastor, what do you need to change and what must you begin to do in order to become your own sermon illustration?
- Can you think of seven to nine men (young and old) who might be learning the value of prayer because they are watching your life? How will you restructure your personal prayer times to include intercession for them to become valiant men of prayer following your example?

Creative Activities
- Preach on "Epaphras: Prayer Warrior" (from Colossians 4:12-13).
- Take a group of men on a retreat that combines recreation (men crave action), study (unpack your sermon on Epaphras), and prayer ("Lord, what will it take to turn us into prayer warriors?").

Strategy 5 — The Mentor

GENERALS NEED CAPTAINS. Every pastor must select, train, and disciple a man who not only can serve (and pray) alongside him but also can cast a vision and lead other men with passion (see 2 Timothy 2:2). This, dear Barnabas, is your Saul who needs to be transformed into a Paul (see Acts 12:25; 13:6-9). This, General Paul, is your Timothy who must become your captain in Ephesus (see 1 Timothy 1:3). You will need to call all men—young and old, mature and new to the faith—to prayer, but ask the Holy Spirit to point out those who have the calling, gifting, and anointing to become vision casters and passionate leaders.

Crucial Questions
- Pastor, has the Lord revealed the Sauls in your ministry who have the potential of becoming Pauls? How many Timothys are you praying for as you mentor them?
- Could you be more effective in the next twelve months at mobilizing the men of your congregation if you were to read a book on the dynamics of mentoring? What can you do in this next year to improve your mentoring and discipling skills?

Creative Activities
- Invite your Sauls and Timothys to meet with you regularly (at least once a month) so that you can mentor them into deeper personal prayer and in prayer leadership skills.
- Take several men to a prayer conference. Build in some "guy time" as well as debriefing: "How can we bless our church (or men's ministry) with what we have learned?"

Strategy 6 — The Ministry

TO CALL YOUR men to war on their knees, should you create a new ministry that has a focus on prayer, or should you bring a new focus on prayer to existing ministries? Answer: yes!

Pray for direction on what additional activity might enable more men to experience the adventure of prayer. But also pray for discernment on how to bring prayer to the places where men are already gathering, whether for ministry, study, work, or recreation.

Crucial Questions
- Pastor, if you were a member (and not the pastor) of your church, what would have to happen for you to take the plunge and attend a men's prayer meeting?
- Who needs to issue the call? Who should be invited? Who should lead?
- What makes this meeting unique? challenging? fulfilling?
- Where is a location that feels like a place where men would open up and really pray? The gym before a game of volleyball or basketball? A corporate conference room? A jogging or hiking trail? Your van parked by the commuter train before they leave for the city?
- When is a time that adds to the challenge? 5:30 A.M. on a weekday? 7:00 A.M. in your study (or office) on Sunday? Surprisingly, men respond to unusual times.
- Why is this a good use of their time?
- How will you use peer influence to get men to the place of prayer?

Creative Activities
- List every event, activity, ministry, and meeting that men participate in throughout a normal church year. After each one, list how prayer can become more of a value in that setting and what you will do to make it happen. Below are some examples of what you could do for men's prayer in different categories.

In their homes:
- Challenge husbands to pray with their wives every day for at least two minutes during the next thirty days. Meet to debrief. A good discussion starter is "What did God have us pray that we have not prayed before?"
- Ask fathers to pray for their children for a week, then pray over each child in the Sunday morning service (invite them to the front of the congregation).

For you, the pastor:
- Challenge men to commit to pray for you while at work, perhaps one specified day a week.
- Invite them to meet with you on Monday mornings to pray for next Sunday's sermon.
- Create a group that communicates prayer requests through e-mail.
- Encourage them to fast and pray for you as they skip a meal once a week.
- Have from seven to twelve men gather around you on Sunday mornings before the service. This "Sunday Prayer Huddle" group could meet for one month, then rotate with another group.

During church services:
- Equip the ushers to pray before services (for gifts of hospitality), during services (to bless each person they serve), and after services (for visitors and those who are hurting or absent).

In the community:

- On the day when kids are praying at school through the See You at the Pole program (usually the second or third Wednesday of September), have fathers stop at their local school before they go to work to stand in support of their children at the largest prayer meeting in the world.[2]
- Ask men to meet at the church, pray for God's presence and protection, then travel to locations in the community that are enveloped by evil or by spiritual darkness. Spend an hour walking, praying, blessing, and inviting the Lord to reign in the schools, the stores, and the homes. See the problems, but pray the promises!

Men's ministry functions:

- Challenge the men to devote from ten to fifteen minutes to pray for one another either before or after each men's Bible study.
- Hold a yearly men's retreat at which you make prayer the theme. Invite a prayer facilitator to colead the retreat with you. You can teach and let the guest guide the group into new prayer experiences.
- Ask men to choose a prayer partner ("tele-friend") whom they will "meet" on the phone once a week so that they can pray for each other, their families, the pastor, the church, and the community.

A true, biblical call to war is much more than a longer message or a louder sermon next Sunday. It is a call that must first be heard and deeply felt by the pastor. It is a call that must come through his life, his teaching, and his leading. For boys to become men in prayer, they must watch and listen to the prayers of their pastor and the men he prays into leadership. When your men hear you pray like Jesus, they will want to spend time with Jesus and talk with the One who prayed "with loud cries and tears to the one who could bring victory in the battle. And he was heard" (Hebrews 5:7, my paraphrase).

EFFECTIVE PRAYER GROUP FACTORS

Dan Erickson

Jesus, the ideal leader, understood the compelling force of small groups. His leadership of only twelve disciples resulted in the birth of a history-shaping global movement. Now that's a powerful force! As twenty-first-century leaders, we also can see our prayer groups propel men to impact their worlds. Just think of the remarkable possibilities for your prayer group!

In our uprooted society, men have a basic need to belong, not to an undifferentiated mob, but to a company of comrades. Men's prayer groups can help meet this basic need. To build a successful men's prayer group, you will need to consider three major factors: (1) clear purpose and expectations, (2) effective leadership, and (3) a trusting climate.

A Clear Purpose and Expectations

ONE OF THE best moves a leader can make to help men connect with a prayer group is to clarify the purpose for the group's existence.

Without a clear purpose, the men may become frustrated and eventually drop out.

Set your purpose in the beginning and review it from time to time. Clear expectations help reduce the conflict that arises when group members have different agendas. Establish the prayer focus for the group. Is it to pray for the pastor and the church's ministries? Is it to pray for the city? The purpose may simply be to enjoy God's presence together as brothers.

Be sure the purpose is clearly understood. For individual members to perform effectively within the group, they must know and own the group goals. If your prayer focus is international missions, someone with an intense burden for local high schools will be frustrated and should probably find another prayer group.

Be relevant, not religious. The group must address the felt needs of its members. Without relevance, the men will lose interest in the group. Regardless of the group's prayer focus, always allow ample time to pray over the men's personal needs.

Understanding and articulating God's purpose for the prayer gathering is critical for success.

Effective Leadership

DIRECTING THE GROUP'S energy toward united prayer calls for skillful leadership. The leader who senses the needs of the group and helps create an environment of trust will bind the group together. Effective leaders help members understand the group dynamics that contribute to or interfere with the success of the prayer meeting.

A men's small group leader is a facilitator. A good facilitator exhibits the following characteristics that will stimulate involvement and give each participant a sense of being a key contributor to the group's success.

- He sees each person as having worth and value. He encourages others in the group to use their gifts.
- He does not force people to speak or pray, but he helps and trains the men to pray aloud.
- He promotes an atmosphere of acceptance and openness.

- He is flexible and sensitive to the needs of the group. He has a warm, understanding, and relaxed manner.
- He is not manipulative but takes the lead without dominating.

The following are leadership skills that are essential to effectively building trust within the prayer group.

- Sensitivity to God—being able to perceive God's leading and guidance during prayer meetings
- Empathy—seeing the world through the eyes of others
- Acceptance—being there for others, though not always approving their actions
- Genuineness—being real rather than phony, not hiding behind religious roles or facades, letting others know the "person inside"
- Emotion—not being afraid to express or pray with emotion and allowing others to express what they feel
- Confrontation—challenging others responsibly and directly but with kindness
- Openness—inviting others to help him change

The stronger the leader, the more powerful the prayer meeting can become.

A Trusting Climate

THE THIRD KEY success factor for a men's prayer group is a climate of trust. How does a leader develop an environment of trust in the prayer meeting?

Elements of a trusting climate. On the human level, risk-taking, support, sensitivity, acceptance, and self-disclosure are some of the key elements that build a trusting climate. But cohesion is probably the strongest element.

The process in which group members are attracted to each other, motivated to remain together, and share a common perspective on the group's activity is called "cohesion." When cohesion is missing, feelings of alienation and irrelevance tend to draw the energy from

FIGHT ON YOUR KNEES

both the individual members and the group as a whole. The sense of togetherness, more than anything else, gives energy to the group. On a spiritual level, the presence of God must be prayed for and expected. Nothing brings cohesion quite like a group of men being changed together in His presence.

Attitudes that create a trusting climate. The attitudes that members bring into the group will either enhance or detract from building and maintaining a trusting prayer environment. The following are positive attitudes that men should bring into the group in order to build a trusting climate.

- Genuineness: Members must desire to be real, not to hide and not to be phony. Honest self-disclosure will usually draw the group together.
- Expectations: Each member should expect the best of what the group has to offer. Participants need to believe that the group experience will be beneficial to them or they will stop attending.
- Cooperation: Each member should work with the others toward achieving the group's purpose and expectations.
- Openness to change: The success of a group depends to a great degree on the members' openness to being changed by the Lord.

The Prayer Meeting

HERE ARE THREE guidelines to help make your prayer group a fulfilling experience.

1. Make prayer as natural as possible. Along this line, William Carr Peel gives the following practical suggestions to men.

Speak to God in simple words and in a conversational tone. You are with your Father and brothers, not in a pulpit. Avoid formal, stiff, or religious language that you don't use in everyday family life. Speak to God as you would to a warm, loving Father, not some austere, distant deity. . . .

Listen! Don't plan ahead what you will say. Join in the prayer as you would a conversation. Your response can be as simple as "Yes, Lord, I agree." . . .

Pray honestly for yourself. Use "I" and "me" when referring to yourself rather than collective nouns, "we" and "us." Don't editorialize. Make it personal. . . .

Pray for things that really concern your heart. A good rule of thumb is to limit group prayer to the issues you are willing to pray about personally. If your concern is not strong enough to spend your own time praying, you should not occupy the time of the group. . . .

Make your requests as specific as possible. What specific sin are you struggling with? What specific way do you want God to bless your friend? What particular action do you want God to take?[1]

2. *Avoid common prayer-group killers.* Harvey Cozzens observed the following six practices in declining and weak prayer groups:

- more talking than praying
- "ball hogs" dominating the prayer time
- quickly jumping from one prayer focus to another
- rushing into the Lord's presence without ample time for men to clear their thoughts and get in tune with Him
- making prayer a heavy burden or duty and not a joy
- allowing controversial discussions before prayer begins[2]

3. *Cultivate an atmosphere of worship and the Word.* Successful prayer meetings mingle worship and praise before and during the prayer meeting. Faith is built when we focus on the greatness of God. Spontaneous songs (sung without instruments) can be a dynamic addition to prayer meetings. If you don't have a worship leader, then use CDs or cassettes. Men are transformed in God's presence; this is more than an emotional sensation. When men have an awareness of the reality of God, their faith is released and their hearts become tender.

Sharing the Bible also builds faith (see Romans 10:17). Incorporate the Scriptures as much as possible. Use the Bible as a prayer book. Find verses that relate to the prayer requests as much as possible.

Worship and the Word will give your prayer meeting a strong foundation of faith.

Real Ministry

UNDERSTANDING HOW GOD wired men as they connect with small groups will help you sustain men's prayer ministries. Nevertheless, following these principles doesn't mean you can automatically program a climate of trust in a prayer group. But it will help immensely. For example, the freedom to express feelings opens the door for trust to grow. And a transparent leader is critical to setting the tone for humility and honesty in the prayer times. The bottom line is that real ministry flows out of trusting relationships, and trusting relationships are produced in a trusting climate. This is our target, because real ministry means men are genuinely touching God. Father is waiting to meet with His sons. Let's go for it!

NOTES

Chapter One: Let Freedom Ring

1. Quoted in Stephen Mansfield, *Never Give In: The Extraordinary Character of Winston Churchill* (Nashville: Cumberland House, 1995), p. 85.
2. Quoted in Stephen W. Anderson, ed., *The Great American Bathroom Book,* vol. 1 (Salt Lake City: Compact Classics, 1991), p. 199.
3. Dutch Sheets, *Praying for America* (Ventura, Calif.: Regal, 2001), pp. 19-20.
4. Mansfield, p. 137.
5. Quoted in Mansfield, p. 71.
6. Quoted in Anderson, p. 197.
7. R. Laird Harris, ed., Gleason L. Archer, Jr. and Bruce K. Waltke, assoc. eds., *Theological Wordbook of the Old Testament,* vol. 2 (Chicago: Moody Press, 1980), p. 939.
8. Harris, p. 594.
9. Harris, p. 773.
10. Edward K. Rowell, ed., *Fresh Illustrations for Preaching and Teaching* (Grand Rapids, Mich.: Baker, 1997), p. 179.
11. Rowell, p. 146.
12. Harris, pp. 594, 773, 939.
13. Quoted in Anderson, p. 200.
14. Craig Brian Larson, *Illustrations for Preaching and Teaching* (Grand Rapids, Mich.: Baker, 1993), p. 280.

Chapter Three: A Soldier's Entanglements

1. John Piper, *A Hunger for God: Desiring God Through Fasting and Prayer* (Wheaton, Ill.: Crossway, 1997), p. 14.
2. Quoted in Dotson Rader, "It Was Time to Act Like a Man," *Parade,* October 8, 2000, p. 8, emphasis added.
3. Dr. Ron Rand, letter to author, March 31, 1995.
4. G. Richard Blackaby, quoted in *Bulletin on Revival* 83. "Corporate Hindrances to Revival," *Revival Commentary Newsletter* 2. no. 2 (1997): pp.6-7.

Chapter Four: Warring for the Foundations

1. The Foundations of Integrity for Authentic Success chart is available at www.thewpc.org.
2. For more information, visit www.calltowar.com.
3. M.A.N. Ministries, "The Crisis in American Males," photocopy.
4. "Crisis in American Males."
5. Bill Hybels, *Honest to God? Becoming an Authentic Christian* (Grand Rapids, Mich.: Zondervan, 1990), p. 12.
6. Gordon Dalbey, "Searching for the Real Men's Movement," *New Man*, September–October 2000, p. 41.
7. Derek Prince, *Husbands and Fathers: Rediscover the Creator's Purpose for Men* (Grand Rapids, Mich.: Chosen Books, 2000), p. 32.
8. Quoted by Tony Evans, sermon at New Life Church, Colorado Springs, Colo., September 20, 2001.
9. Nancy R. Gibbs, "Bringing Up Father," *Time*, June 28, 1993, p. 55.
10. Quoted in Paul Lewis, *The Five Key Habits of Smart Dads* (Grand Rapids, Mich.: Zondervan, 1994), p. 24.
11. Go to www.theamen.org for more information.
12. "Evangelical Christians," Gallup Research Corporation Summary Report, May 1991, quoted in Cheri Fuller, *When Couples Pray: The Little-Known Secret to Lifelong Happiness in Marriage* (Sisters, Oreg.: Multnomah, 2001), p. 12.
13. *The Hour That Changes the World* video series by Dick Eastman (available at www.thewpc.org) has been very effective for training our children to spend an hour with God daily.
14. Two excellent resources are Gary Smalley and John Trent, *The Blessing* (Nashville: Nelson, 1986); and Randy and Lisa Wilson, *Daddy's Blessing* (Colorado Springs, Colo.: Cook Communications, 1997).
15. The Get Real Planner is a creative tool to help you write your family mission statement and ninety-day goals and evaluate your 168 hours per week. It is available at www.thewpc.org.
16. Lewis, pp. 84-85.
17. Dennis Rainey, *One Home at a Time: Restoring the Soul of America Through God's Plan for Your Marriage and Family* (Wheaton, Ill.: Tyndale, 1997), pp. 32-33.
18. Joe Maxwell, "Men Are Back," *New Man*, September–October 2000, p. 35.
19. Maxwell, p. 35.

Chapter Five: Ensuring Domestic Tranquility

1. Quoted in Cheri Fuller, *When Couples Pray: The Little-Known Secret to Lifelong Happiness in Marriage* (Sisters, Oreg.: Multnomah, 2001), p. 52.

2. I am indebted for this insight to Mell Winger, "Restoring a Vision for the Small Prayer Meeting," *Connected,* October 2001, p. 1.

3. Fuller, p. 36.

4. Edwin Louis Cole, *Strong Men in Tough Times* (Lake Mary, Fla.: Creation House, 1993), p. 154.

5. Beth Moore, *Praying God's Word: Breaking Free from Spiritual Strongholds* (Nashville: Broadman, 2000), pp. 59-60.

6. Warren and Ruth Myers, *Thirty-One Days of Prayer: Moving God's Mighty Hand* (Sisters, Oreg.: Multnomah, 1997), p. 162.

7. Myers, p. 164.

8. Quoted in Myers, p. 80.

9. Fuller, p. 66.

10. Lou Priolo, *The Complete Husband: A Practical Guide to Biblical Husbanding* (Amityville, N.Y.: Calvary Press, 1999), p. 10.

11. Shmuley Boteach, *Kosher Sex: A Recipe for Passion and Intimacy* (New York: Doubleday, 1999), p. 276.

12. Ron Mehl, *Ten(der) Commandments: Reflections on the Father's Love* (Sisters, Oreg.: Multnomah, 1998), pp.188-189.

13. Randy and Lisa Wilson, *Celebrations of Faith* (Colorado Springs, Colo.: Cook Communications, 2001), p. 109.

14. *The Complete Churchill,* BBC, 1991, videocassette.

Chapter Six: The Legacy of a Praying Father

1. Cheri Fuller, *When Mothers Pray* (Sisters, Oreg.: Multnomah, 1997), p. 88.

2. Dick Eastman, *Love on Its Knees* (Old Tappan, N.J.: Chosen Books, 1989), pp. 151-153.

3. Eastman, pp. 152-153.

4. Joe White and Jim Weidmann, eds., *Parents' Guide to the Spiritual Mentoring of Teens* (Wheaton, Ill.: Tyndale, 2001), p. 422.

5. White and Weidmann, p. 422.

6. Richard Foster, *Prayer: Finding the Heart's True Home* (San Francisco: HarperSanFrancisco, 1992), p. 176.

7. Randy and Lisa Wilson, *Celebrations of Faith: Tying Your Children's Heartstrings to God's Truth* (Colorado Springs, Colo.: Cook Communications, 2001).

8. Joyce Meyer, "Practical Ways to Walk in Love," *Life in the Word,* February 2002, p. 5.

9. O. Hallesby, *Prayer* (Minneapolis: Augsburg, 1959), p. 174.

Chapter Seven: Lifestyle Warfare

1. William Barclay, *The Letters to the Philippians, Colossians, and Thessalonians* (Edinburgh: Saint Andrew Press, 1961), p. 130.

2. Charles H. Kraft and Mark White, eds., *Behind Enemy Lines: An Advanced Guide to Spiritual Warfare* (Ann Arbor, Mich.: Servant, 1994), pp. 18-21.

3. C. Peter Wagner, *Warfare Prayer: How to Seek God's Power and Protection in the Battle to Build His Kingdom* (Ventura, Calif.: Regal, 1992), p. 61.

4. James Kallas, *The Real Satan: From Biblical Times to the Present* (Minneapolis: Augsburg, 1975), p. 60.

5. John Wimber, *Power Evangelism* (San Francisco: Harper & Row, 1986), p. 13.

6. Quoted in Dick Eastman, *Change the World School of Prayer Instructors Manual,* rev. ed., fall 1993, p. 24.

Chapter Eight: Skills and Weapons of War

1. Charles Spurgeon, *Twelve Sermons on Prayer* (Grand Rapids, Mich.: Baker, 1971), p. 14.

2. Quoted in Beth Alves, *The Mighty Warrior* (Bulverde, Tex.: Intercessors International, 1987), p. 97.

3. Gary Kinnaman, *Overcoming the Dominion of Darkness: Personal Strategies for Spiritual Warfare* (Old Tappan, N.J.: Chosen Books, 1990), p. 134.

4. Jack Hayford, *Prayer Is Invading the Impossible* (New York: Ballantine, 1983), pp. 123-124.

5. Richard Foster, *Prayer: Finding the Heart's True Home* (San Francisco: HarperSanFrancisco, 1992), p. 99.

6. Jack Taylor, *The Hallelujah Factor* (Nashville: Broadman, 1983), p. 33.

7. C. S. Lewis, *The Screwtape Letters* (New York: Macmillan, 1962), p. 3.

8. Hayford, p. 16.

Chapter Nine: Men Under Authority

1. Mario Murillo, *Critical Mass: A Strategy for a North American Revival* (Chatsworth, Calif.: Anthony Douglas Publishing, 1985), p. xi.

2. Charles Ryrie, *Ryrie Study Bible Expanded Edition,* NASB 1995

Update (Chicago: Moody), p. 1287.

3. John Bevere, sermon at the World Prayer Center, Colorado Springs, Colo., February 20, 2002.

4. Gary D. Kinnaman, *Overcoming the Dominion of Darkness: Personal Strategies for Spiritual Warfare* (Old Tappan, N.J.: Chosen Books, 1990), p. 69.

5. C. Peter Wagner, *Prayer Shield: How to Intercede for Pastors, Christian Leaders, and Others on the Spiritual Frontlines* (Ventura, Calif.: Gospel Light/Regal, 1992), p. 61.

6. Wagner, p. 73.

7. Terry Teykl, *Preyed On or Prayed For?* (Muncie, Ind.: Prayer Point Press, 2000), front cover.

8. Mell Winger, "Wisdom, Walk, and Work: An Apostolic Prayer for Pastors," *Empowered!* fall 2001, pp. 12-13.

9. Wagner, inside cover.

10. Chuck Kraft, *Deep Wounds, Deep Healing: Discovering the Vital Link Between Spiritual Warfare and Inner Healing* (Ann Arbor, Mich.: Servant, 1993), p. 84.

Chapter Ten: The Warrior's Heart

1. John Wimber, *Power Evangelism* (San Francisco: Harper & Row, 1986), p. 8.

2. John Eldredge, *Wild at Heart: Discovering the Passionate Soul of a Man* (Nashville: Nelson, 2001), pp. 140-141.

3. Francis Frangipane, *The Three Battlegrounds* (Marion, Iowa: Advancing Church Publications, 1989), pp. 9,13.

4. Frangipane, p. 46.

5. Frangipane, p. 4.

6. I owe this idea to Doug Giles, sermon at His People, Miami, Fla., January 28, 2001.

7. Frederick E. Hoxie with Frank Rzeczkowski, *Grapevine Creek Battle* (Crow Tribal Council, Crow Agency, Montana, and the Department of the Interior, National Park Service, Intermountain Support Office, Denver, Colo., undated), pp. 38-39.

Chapter Eleven: The Warrior's Identity

1. Robert L. Thomas, ed., *New American Standard Exhaustive Concordance of the Bible* (Nashville: Holman, 1981), p. 1585.

2. Thomas, pp. 1528, 1562.

3. Thomas, pp. 1528, 1606.

4. Thomas, p. 1502.
5. Robert Hicks, *The Masculine Journey: Understanding the Six Stages of Manhood* (Colorado Springs, Colo.: NavPress, 1993), p. 23.
6. Hicks, p. 24
7. Hicks, p. 25.
8. Hicks, p. 25.
9. Hicks, p. 26.
10. Hicks, pp. 27-28.

Conclusion: Call to War

1. S. D. Gordon, *Quiet Talks on Prayer* (New York: Grosset & Dunlap, 1904), p. 27.
2. Dick Eastman, *Change the World School of Prayer Basic Manual,* 1991, p. D-85.
3. *A Call to War,* prod. Derek Packard, World Prayer Center, November 27, 2001, videocassette.
4. Paul Billheimer, *The Technique of Spiritual Warfare* (Santa Ana, Calif.: TBN Press, 1982), p. 58.

Appendix One: Pastors' Strategies for Mobilizing Men to Pray

1. To find a book about prayer, check out www.navpress.com/praymag.asp. To locate a prayer training conference, go to www.nalcpl.net. To find a pastors' prayer group, search www.nppn.org/ppg.
2. To learn more about the See You at the Pole program, go to www.syatp.com.

Appendix Two: Effective Prayer Group Factors

1. William Carr Peel, *What God Does When Men Pray* (Colorado Springs, Colo.: NavPress, 1993), pp. 45-47.
2. Harvey Cozzens, "Nurturing or Quenching a Prayer Group," *Connected,* August 2001, pp. 4-5.

ABOUT THE CONTRIBUTORS

JIM CHOSA pastors Church in the Wilderness in the heart of the Crow Nation at Yellowtail, Montana. He and his wife, Faith, minister all over the United States, building networks between the native and nonnative cultures within the church.

HARVEY COZZENS is president of the Oxford Lamb Foundation and is a real estate broker and developer in Colorado Springs. He and his wife of thirty-one years, Priscilla, have two adult sons: Nathan, a pilot in the U.S. Air Force; and Chris, a missionary and professional hunting guide.

DAN ERICKSON is the executive director of the National Coalition of Men's Ministries (NCMM), based in Lee's Summit, Missouri. He and his wife, Cathy, have been married thirty-one years. They have two children and two grandchildren. (To learn about NCMM, visit their Web site at www.ncmm.org.)

GEOFF GORSUCH is the executive director of men's ministries for the Navigators. He was instrumental in the development of the National Coalition of Men's Ministries. Geoff flew more than one hundred combat missions in Vietnam as a reconnaissance pilot. For his meritorious service, he was awarded the Silver Star and four Distinguished Flying Crosses. He resides in Colorado with his wife, Diane. They have two grown daughters.

TED HAGGARD is the founder and senior pastor of the nine-thousand-member New Life Church in Colorado Springs. He is the author of *Primary Purpose, Letters from Home,* and *The Life-Giving Church.* He coauthored *Loving Your City into the Kingdom* with Jack Hayford and *Confident Parent, Exceptional Teens* with John Bolin. Ted and his wife, Gayle, have five children.

CALVIN JOHNSON lives in Colorado Springs with his wife, Debra, and two teenage sons, Bryan and Calvin, Jr. Calvin is the senior pastor of Solid Rock Christian Church, a multicultural body of believers who are committed to war for the souls of people and to equip disciples to fulfill their destiny.

BILL MCCARTNEY is the founder and president of Promise Keepers. He was an award-winning football coach at the University of Colorado from 1982 to 1995. He and his wife, Lyndi, live in the Denver area. They have four children and eight grandchildren.

PHIL MIGLIORATTI is the director of the National Pastors' Prayer Network (NPPN). He is a member of the National Prayer Committee and is national cities facilitator for Mission America. Phil pastored for twenty years. He and his wife, Carol, live in Palatine, Illinois. They have two married daughters. (For more information on NPPN, visit their Web site at www.nppn.org.)

DEREK PACKARD, director of the A-Men Project, is an award-winning director and producer. Using live satellite broadcasts, the A-Men Project helps local churches train men in prayer and discipleship. He and his wife, Marie, have two young daughters. (To learn about the A-Men Project, visit www.theamen.org.)

DALE SCHLAFER is the founder and president of the Center for World Revival and Awakening. He pastored for twenty-eight years and served on the staff of Promise Keepers. He and his wife, Liz, have three grown children. They live in Colorado.

STEVE SHANKLIN is a senior partner of Destiny Consultants, which specializes in nonprofit management. Formerly, he served as the national network prayer manager for Promise Keepers. He is the author of *The Book of Prayers: A Man's Guide to Reaching God*. He and his wife, Denise, and their sons live in the Houston area.

DUTCH SHEETS is the senior pastor of Springs Harvest Fellowship in Colorado Springs. He travels extensively, teaching and ministering primarily on prayer and revival. He is the author of several books, including the best-selling *Intercessory Prayer*. He and his wife, Ceci, have two daughters, Sarah and Hannah. (For more information, visit his Web site at www.dutchsheets.org.)

WESLEY TULLIS is the pastor of prayer at New Life Church in Colorado Springs, as well as the director of the World Prayer Center. Wes developed key ministries for the U.S. Center for World Mission, Youth With a Mission, and Every Home for Christ. Wes and his wife, Sandi, have six children.

RANDY WILSON is a father of seven and has been married to Lisa for twenty years. He works in legislative and cultural affairs at Focus on the Family and is the founder of Generations of Light Ministries. He and his wife have written three books: *Celebrations of Faith, Daddy's Blessing,* and *The Joshua Basket.*

ABOUT THE EDITOR

DR. MELL WINGER is a teacher, author, and former pastor and missionary. He is currently director of church relations for the National Association of Local Church Prayer Leaders (NALCPL), a ministry of the World Prayer Center in Colorado Springs, Colorado.

Dr. Winger pastored in Texas for ten years before moving to Colorado Springs and joining the staff of the international missions organization Every Home for Christ. He spent three years developing a leadership institute to train pastors and missionaries in Guatemala City, Guatemala.

He and his wife, Paula, have two sons, Andrew and Joseph, and a daughter, Elizabeth.

"*Fight on Your Knees* sounds reveille on a veritable trumpet from heaven aimed at waking the troops up, getting them out of bed, taking up their spiritual weapons, and charging out to the battlefield. We can win the war for the kingdom of God if only Christian men all over the world will hear this sound and resolutely begin marching to its beat!"
— C. Peter Wagner, chancellor, Wagner Leadership Institute

"What a refreshing approach to strategic living and praying! It richly expands on Matthew 11:12: 'The Kingdom of God is forcefully advancing, and people of force are laying hold of it.' Let it expand your involvement in the triumphs of Christ right where you serve Him. Every chapter summons you: 'Rise up, O men of God. Have done with lesser things. Give heart and mind and soul and strength to serve the King of Kings.'"
— David Bryant, president, Concerts of Prayer International; chairman, America's National Prayer Committee; director, Proclaim Hope!

"No one could be better qualified to assemble this wonderful collection of inspirational articles than my friend Mell Winger, whose life radiates a deep and genuine relationship with God. This book is a wealth of thoughtful reflections on a subject everyone seems to be talking about lately: prayer. Read this book and deepen your understanding of communion with God, but more, catch the passion of men who are uniquely gifted to stir us to pray."
— Dr. Gary Kinnaman, senior minister, Word of God Church, Mesa, Arizona

"In this book, you will hear the hearts of known and trusted men of God, leaders in the body of Christ, issue a clarion call for men to rise to their God-given destinies as spiritual warriors through the power of prayer. Filled with biblical insight as well as practical application for deepening a man's prayer life, this book is a great tool for husbands, fathers, and sons—one that will challenge and help men to answer the call."
— Jane Hansen, president/CEO, Aglow International